• A HISTORY LOVER'S •
GUIDE TO
NEW HAMPSHIRE

•A HISTORY LOVER'S•
GUIDE TO
NEW HAMPSHIRE

KATHLEEN D. BAILEY & SHEILA R. BAILEY

THE
History
PRESS

Published by The History Press
Charleston, SC
www.historypress.com

First published 2025

Manufactured in the United States

ISBN 9781467155984

Library of Congress Control Number: 2024949763

Notice: The information in this book is true and complete to the best of our knowledge. It is offered without guarantee on the part of the author or The History Press. The author and The History Press disclaim all liability in connection with the use of this book.

I would like to dedicate this book to my daughter and coauthor, Sheila R. Bailey. She was a joyful participant on our four Arcadia books: *Past and Present Exeter, New Hampshire, New Hampshire War Monuments: The Stories Behind the Stones, Growing Up in Concord, New Hampshire: Boomer Memories from White's Park to the Capitol Theater* and *A History Lover's Guide to New Hampshire.* We had many adventures as we trolled the Granite State looking for the perfect shot. From driving past Derrick Oxford's grave three times (*War Monuments*) to hanging out a three-story window (*Exeter*) to hunting down the Lost Village of Monson (*History Lover's*), we got lost a lot and chased our goals through heat, cold and COVID.

She relished seeing our books on bookstore shelves and enjoyed signings and promotional events. We will never forget her, and because of the books, you don't need to either.

To Sheila Rose Bailey (August 13, 1981–June 14, 2024)

CONTENTS

ACKNOWLEDGEMENTS

I am indebted to:

NORTH COUNTRY:
Berlin, Renney Morneau, photos and reflections on his city.
Berlin, Pamela LaFlamme, director of strategic initiatives for the city.
Berlin and the North Country, Ericka Canales, former executive director, Coos Economic Development Corporation.
Berlin, Dr. Linda Upham-Bornstein, material on town history website.
Bethlehem, David Goldstone, Bethlehem Hebrew Congregation.
Bethlehem, Linda Herrman, reminiscences of the hotel era.
Bethlehem, Mike Dickerman, permission to quote from his book coauthored with Gregory C. Wilson, *Bethlehem, New Hampshire, 1999 Bicentennial Edition*, published by Bondcliff Books. I used material from sections contributed by Sarah Masur and Ruth Pactor.
Bethlehem, Clare Brown, interview and photos.
The Old Woman, hiker Lexi Broucam, interview.
The Old Woman, John Compton, the Happy Hiker, photo.
The Rocks, Nigel Manley, photographs and interview.

THE WHITE MOUNTAINS:
Indian Head and Old Woman, Carol Riley, president, Upper Pemi Historical Society, background.
Littleton, Veronica Francis, interview and photos.
Littleton, Richard and Debbie Alberini, interview and photos.

THE LAKES REGION:
Castle in the Clouds, Charles Clark, photos and interview.
Laconia Daily Sun, permission to quote from two articles about Roy Small.

DARTMOUTH/LAKE SUNAPEE:
The Fells, former education director Simon Parsons, photos and interview.
The Saint-Gaudens National Historic Site, supervisory park ranger Kerstin Burlingame, photos and interview.

MONADNOCK REGION:
Historic Harrisville, former executive director Erin Hammerstedt, photos and background material.
Madame Sherri Forest, Chesterfield Historical Society, photos; Lynne Borofsky, video; "American Ruins" video; Matt Scaccia, Forest Society, background information.

CONCORD/FRANKLIN PIERCE:
Alfred Perron archives, Pierce Brigade historic photos.
Pierce Homestead, Sara Dobrowolski, tour and background.
Pierce Manse, Kat Braden, tour and photos.
State of New Hampshire, photos.

SEACOAST:
Moffatt-Ladd House, Lauren Gianino, guided tour.
Warner House, Stephanie Hewson, guided tour.
Wentworth-Gardner House, Mary Sullivan, guided tour.

MANCHESTER/NASHUA:
The Millyards, Jeffrey Barraclough, executive director, Millyard Museum, interview.
The Millyards, photos, Library of Congress.
Lost Village of Monson, Matt Scaccia, Forest Society, background and photos.
Nashua Dodgers, Steve Daly, author, *Dem Little Bums* (Concord, NH: Plaidswede Publishing, 1993).
Nashua Dodgers, Barbara Ward, Black Heritage Trail, interview.
Nashua Dodgers, Michael Atkins, executive council, Greater Nashua NAACP, interview.

CONCORD AREA:
Canterbury Shaker Village, Alfred Perron archives.
Mount Kearsarge Indian Museum, Andrew Bullock, photos and history.
Life of Bud Thompson, Darryl Thompson, photos and memories.

ALSO:
My editor Michael Kinsella. This was Sheila's and my fourth book with Arcadia and our third with Michael. Mike, you need to start screening your calls!
My coauthor, Sheila R. Bailey. What a wild ride it has been. We will never forget you.
My family—my husband, David, and daughter Autumn Kent—for their support.
And the many Granite Staters who drew back the curtain to tell us these great stories.

INTRODUCTION

New Hampshire is not like other places, for better or worse.

A diplomat, an artist and an industrialist all found a home in New Hampshire and left a legacy. Two talented pro baseball players found acceptance, despite the color of their skin. Another group of people, the Hasidic Jews, found refuge in a small mountain town.

The list goes on. Famous authors from J.D. Salinger to Tomie de Paola found they could live here, go to the supermarket or the gas station and be left alone. We know who you are, but so what? Salinger's Cornish continues to protect him, even after his death. Don't be surprised if you get a "J.D. who?" when you ask about his old house. Better yet, don't ask at all.

New Hampshire is a place where people can chase their dreams or find them in the first place. Charles "Bud" Thompson was a traveling folk singer with a young family when he stopped at the Canterbury Shaker complex, where he remained for half a lifetime. With the help of the remaining Shaker sisters, he rebuilt the complex into one of the foremost village museums in the Northeast. But Thompson wasn't done yet, and in his seventies, he fulfilled a lifelong dream of opening a museum honoring Native American culture. He didn't have a degree in museum studies; he just did it. And New Hampshire helped.

New Hampshire is a place where people can be safe. In the eighteenth, nineteenth and early twentieth centuries, New Hampshire was a deeply conservative place. Homegrown Yankees, honed by making a living out of the rocks, spoke their minds (and gave bad directions to people from "away"). The French Canadians who came down from Canada to work in the mills were also a conservative people, defined by faith and family. Other immigrants, who fled poverty in Europe, hung on to what was theirs. They voted to the right and colored within the lines. But they also had open minds—if something was worth opening for.

Roy Campanella and Don Newcombe, two young Negro League baseball players, played for the Nashua Dodgers, the first integrated minor-league team, before Jackie Robinson broke the major-league color barrier. Nashua accepted them, inviting them to their living rooms and kitchen tables. The only documented racial incident in their time here was with a team from Lynn, Massachusetts. But Nashua left them alone.

New Hampshire is a place where people think things through. A president's accomplishments are thoughtfully examined by people who see the big picture, even if they don't agree with it. Franklin Pierce wasn't a stellar president. New Hampshire recognizes his faults, shrugs and goes on. Rene Gagnon actually didn't hoist the flag in the classic photograph on Iwo Jima. New Hampshire recognizes his omission, shrugs and goes on. He was still a hero, just not the hero we thought he was. We don't tear down monuments. We recognize flawed individuals, walk around the problem, kick its tires and learn from it.

New Hampshire knows how to use resources and also how to reinvent itself. We built mills and factories, harnessing the power of our mighty rivers. When the mills failed, along with the company-town culture, we found new ways to make things and do things, sometimes within the same classic buildings. Former mill towns continue to battle their way back from shuttered factories and shattered dreams.

New Hampshire knows the right questions to ask. In our storied first-in-the-nation primary, we vet the candidates in living rooms, school gyms and town halls. We're hard to win over but fiercely loyal when you do.

And in the twenty-first century, New Hampshire continues to take care of our own and redefine who "our own" is. We've opened our doors to people who don't look like us. We sample their cultures and cuisines in international festivals or, even better, in their homes or ours. We make it work and learn something along the way.

Welcome to New Hampshire. And if you're really lucky, welcome home.

Chapter 1

BERLIN

WHAT WE LOST, WHAT WE KEPT

Renney Morneau remembers Berlin in the 1960s as a "powerhouse." The only city north of the White Mountains had everything a young boy could want. The economy, fueled by the Brown Company and other large mills, in turn fueled smaller factories and dozens of locally owned businesses. There were small and chain groceries, clothing stores and the triumvirate of five-and-dimes—Woolworth's, J.J. Newberry's and W.T. Grant.

"On Friday nights we'd get dressed up and go downtown," Morneau, now sixty-two, recalls. He especially remembers the hot peanuts from Woolworth's "nut counter," a weekly indulgence. He also enjoyed the French fries at the lunch counter. For other treats, there was Kelly's Pastry Shop and the Northland Dairy Bar, on the road to Milan.

Berlin boasted three first-run movie theaters in the early twentieth century: the Princess, built in 1914; the Albert, built in 1910, which burned and was replaced by W.T. Grant; and the Strand, built in the 1940s and eventually replaced by a bowling alley.

Though Morneau was an only child, he was never lonely, and he roamed the bustling downtown with a pack of friends. "There were," he said, "a lot of kids." In addition to three public elementary schools, Berlin had a junior high and a high school. The Catholic community supported four parochial elementary schools and a high school.

Morneau remembers he and his pals riding their bikes to a nearby hardware store and taking home used cardboard boxes. "We'd make little houses with them," he recalls. They would fly kites in the parking lot of the Brown Company mill. He says, "We had the run of the millyard."

The only place off-limits was a section behind a gate, where the company built what he remembers as "cement igloos" to hold the used timecards. "We would wallow in the igloos," Morneau says. "Our quest was to come out with different colors of timecards" and to do it before the Brown Company guards got there.

The boys also spent their allowances at Andy's Market, Plunkett's Pharmacy and LePage's store, which had an oak counter with penny candy behind its gleaming glass.

Berlin was a good place for children to grow up and for adults to raise them. The mills and the businesses that grew up around them provided excellent pay and benefits.

But Berlin wasn't always BERlin or even BerLINN.

MAYNESBOROUGH

By the time white people knew the rich resources of the city by the river, Native Americans had already staked out a presence near the caves on Mount Jasper, a source for the mineral rhyolite. Rhyolite was essential in crafting Native tools. The mine site is preserved and on the National Register of Historic Places.[1]

The Abenaki also coined the name for the river that would power mills and economies well into the twentieth century: Androscoggin, or "fish-curing place."

Colonial Governor John Wentworth created what was to be New Hampshire's northernmost city in December 1771, when he chartered the town of Maynesborough, after Sir William Maynes, and granted charters of land to his fellow Englishmen. A pesky little thing called the Revolution interfered, and none of the grantees ever took up their claims. Was it too remote? Too wild? Too cold?

Seth Eames and William Tirrell, dispatched by descendants of Mayne, ventured north in 1802 to carve out lots for prospective settlers. The land went unclaimed until 1823 and 1824, when William Sessions and his nephew Cyrus Wheeler, both of Gilead, Maine, finally settled Maynesborough. The first industry was farming. By 1829, the town had sixty-five hardy residents and reincorporated as Berlin after the city of Berlin, Germany, then in the city-state of Prussia. They continued to farm

Left: An early logger brings freshly cut wood to the Brown Company's paper mill. *Michael J. Spinelli Jr. Center for University Archives and Special Collections, Plymouth State University. Brown Collection.*

Below: The front entrance of the Brown Company main building in its heyday. *Michael J. Spinelli Jr. Center for University Archives and Special Collections, Plymouth State University. Brown Collection.*

the rocky terrain until 1852, when everything changed, and the Berlin of the next century took shape.

What changed Berlin? The railroad.

The city had already developed as a center for logging and wood industry, thanks to the power generated by the Androscoggin River. The mighty Androscoggin flows south from Umbagog Lake to Gorham and Berlin, east to Jay, Maine, and then south to the Atlantic Ocean, a total of 175 miles. The two steepest drops are at Berlin and Rumford, Maine. The river powered pulp and paper mills in Berlin; textile factories in Lewiston, Maine; and shoe factories in Auburn, Maine. The introduction of the turbine engine improved the generating of power for the mills.

In 1851, the St. Lawrence and Atlantic Railroad established a line connecting Berlin to the rest of the state—and country. The Boston and Maine Railroad began operating a line in 1874.

The H. Winslow Company saw the potential in the woods and the Androscoggin and bought up the water, timber and rail rights in the early 1850s and then built a large sawmill at the head of Berlin Falls.

In 1868, William Wentworth Brown and Lewis T. Brown (no relation) bought a controlling interest in the company, changing its name to Berlin Mills Company. W.W. Brown and his family acquired the remaining stock in the 1880s. Brown expanded and diversified the business, including chemical, pulp and paper mills.

Other industrialists also took advantage of the technological, transportation and immigration factors. In 1877, H.H. Furbish established Forest Fiber Co., the first chemical pulp mill in Berlin, which he operated until the 1890s. Furbish then turned his interests to the production of electricity for the area with the mill's hydroelectric dam. In 1885, the owners of the *Boston Globe* and the *New York Tribune* built Glen Manufacturing Company, Berlin's first paper mill designed to produce newsprint, which they sold to International Paper Company in 1898.

NORTHERN LIGHTS

By the early twentieth century, Berlin Mills Company, which during World War I had changed its name to Brown Company, had become the most prominent pulp and papermaking operation in Berlin and a leader in the pulp and papermaking industry nationally. In 1915, under the supervision of Hugh K. Moore, Brown Company built a separate research and

Women work in the cutting room at the Brown Company, Berlin. The mill economy made it possible for both genders to enter the workforce. *Michael J. Spinelli Jr. Center for University Archives and Special Collections, Plymouth State University. Brown Collection.*

development facility, the first in the industry. During the 1920s, the Brown Company Research and Development Department employed more than one hundred scientists and technicians, and it produced hundreds of patents. By 1929, Brown Company owned mills from Canada to Florida, employed more than nine thousand men and had assets exceeding $75 million. The Berlin Centennial publication noted that "between 4,000 and 5,000 men [were] needed each winter to supply the mills with 400 thousand cords of wood used every year by the mills." Women were also part of the equation.[2]

With payrolls to fill, the city attracted immigrants from Russia, Norway, Sweden, Finland, Germany and Ireland. French Canadians migrated south from Quebec, and at one time 65 percent of Berlin's residents spoke a form of dialect known as "Berlin French."

With anti-German sentiment rising in the First World War, the canny Yankees north of the Notches knew they had to do something. It would have been a headache and an expense to change all municipal correspondence and signage, so they simply changed the pronunciation of the North's only

The Brown Company store fed the needs of workers. According to historian Raymond Daigle, the store was built in 1853 by the Winslow family, before W.W. Brown bought the sawmill from them. Workers could buy what they needed, put it on credit and pay for it on payday, once a month in the early years. *Michael J. Spinelli Jr. Center for University Archives and Special Collections, Plymouth State University. Brown Collection.*

city. Ber-LINN became BER-linn. The Berlin Mills Company was also renamed the Brown Company.

Berlin's population peaked at twenty thousand in the 1930 census. At the time of the census, 80 percent of Berlin's residents were immigrants or children of immigrants, and 57 percent of the population were French Canadian.

Berlin was the first city in New Hampshire to have electric lights, generated by the Furbish power plant. There were seven banks and three theaters with a combined capacity of 3,650, a symphony orchestra and a band. The new Americans had established their own churches, fraternal organizations and charities, although their shared purpose and those bitter northern winters eventually blurred the edges between cultures, and they were just "Berlin." The schools were good, the pay was high and the outlook was bright.[3]

Then came the Depression. In 1931, International Paper Company closed its doors. It was the first stumble in the fall of Berlin.

Workers from the Brown Company, Berlin's premier paper mill, play basketball on a company team. *Michael J. Spinelli Jr. Center for University Archives and Special Collections, Plymouth State University. Brown Collection.*

The Brown Company would not be the first to be crushed under the anvil of the Depression. The company survived 1929, 1930 and 1931. But by the end of 1931, the international financial crisis had undermined Brown Company's bonds. The company could not finance its winter logging operation in 1931–32.[4]

The company went into receivership shortly after the Great Depression. Bought and sold several times, it underwent bankruptcy again in 1940 and survived until 1968, often with governmental help.

Berlin also survived, if not thrived, for a few more years.

There was relatively little international competition, Morneau says. And the Brown Company's research department was "second to none." He explains, "I had the pleasure of being friends with one of the chemists. He was like an adopted grandfather to me." The man held an astonishing fifty-five chemical patents, Morneau says.

He says now, "They had the best machines, brilliant minds, good marketing strategies."

But it wasn't enough, and Morneau watched the lifestyle slip away. By the 1970s, some of the equipment was out-of-date and some of the processes more labor-intensive, according to him.

Workers from the Brown Company play cards during a break time. *Michael J. Spinelli Jr. Center for University Archives and Special Collections, Plymouth State University. Brown Collection.*

The former Brown Company Research and Development headquarters. *Michael J. Spinelli Jr. Center for University Archives and Special Collections, Plymouth State University. Brown Collection.*

Though Morneau was not to have a career in the mills, he did work there in the summers and remembers working in something called the "digester house." The main purpose of the digester operation was to cook and process wood chips. "We had eight units, and we had to take off the lug nuts with wrenches and check the process," he notes. He was twenty-one and worked alongside an eighty-two-year-old. The older man had to take off the steel covers from a seven-hundred-pound piece of equipment. Morneau was on duty one day when the older man told him, "We're going automatic. It will only take three people per shift." Morneau remembers thinking that the automation would make the company more competitive. "But at the same time, it was the end of the life we'd known."

The Browns were benevolent to the community and supported efforts such as United Way, according to Morneau. They funded sports teams, including a semipro hockey outfit, and they established a visiting nurse system for the town. The later owners? Not so much. One owner fleeced the pension funds. Another company, Crown Vantage, was known colloquially as "Crown Disadvantage," Morneau notes.

The only physical remnant of the Brown Company are two antique barns being restored by the Berlin Coos County Historical Society and the former Brown operations center, now housing several social service agencies.

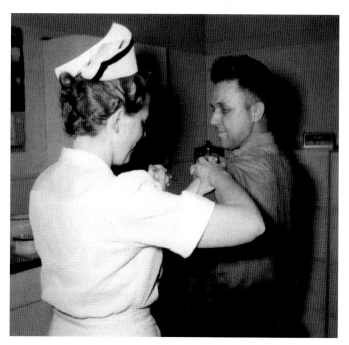

A nurse vaccinates a Brown Company worker. Though the "company store" mentality didn't endure, the company continued to try to meet community needs until it was sold. *Michael J. Spinelli Jr. Center for University Archives and Special Collections, Plymouth State University. Brown Collection.*

The other mills also declined, were acquired by out-of-state owners and eventually closed. The last pulp mill, Fraser Paper, closed its Berlin plant in 2006 but continues to operate its facility in Gorham.

Morneau's daughter was seven at the time of the closure. The final owner of the last mill standing announced they were going to take down the smokestacks, and Morneau took his daughter to the top of Guilmette Street to watch. He videotaped the event, and as the towers came down, "I felt a lump in my throat," he says.

"What were we going to do? Those mills sustained a community," Morneau says.

Morneau was in the state legislature by then, and he remembers U.S. Representative Charlie Bass (R-NH) trying to work with the town. Bass was instrumental in obtaining a biomass plant on one old mill site, which provided some jobs. Another mill, the Cascade Mill, reinvented itself in Cascade, a Berlin suburb, and there were another seventy-five jobs, according to Morneau.

START YOUR ENGINES

The city also increased its tourism efforts and found a partial answer in the ATV craze. A nearby mountain, Jericho Mountain, was "logged out" and no good for the paper trade anymore, if there had been a paper trade. "The closest ATV park was in Virginia," Morneau recalls. The city purchased the land and turned it into Jericho Lake State Park. An annual ATV festival brings people and dollars back into Berlin.

Ericka Canales, former executive director of the Coos County Economic Development Corporation, said that marketing the area had several facets. For the employer, the north is a win, with the cost of land and buildings significantly lower than in the southern tier. The cost of living, including housing, is also lower for those trying to build a blue-collar workforce.

While the north has yet to snag a major employer, small businesses are making a comeback, according to Canales. She cited a new Mexican restaurant, a disc golf center and a bakery/café recently opened on Berlin's Main Street.

The North Country is "an outdoor person's dream," according to Canales. Many people who were accustomed to coming up on weekends have, since remote working took off, made their second homes their primary homes. "They stay and play," she says. There's hunting, fishing, snowmobiling and, of course, the ATV community.

The St. Lawrence Railroad will be passing through the Berlin area on its route from Canada to Maine as part of a $9 million federally funded upgrade. It's necessary to have rail service, according to Canales, because the far north isn't near a Route 93 or 95. The upgraded line will also allow northern businesses to more easily move larger products for export, according to her.

Berlin is open for business, according to the city website, and incentives to employers include a Small Business Administration HUB zone and a downtown tax incentive.[5]

Pamela LaFlamme, director of strategic initiatives for the town, confirms that over the past decade, the city has put a focus on the development of outdoor recreation and the ATV trade. But they are also concentrating on other types of business, such as a multi-acre greenhouse. With the help of grants, they've made a concerted effort to make Berlin shine again, including, in LaFlamme's words, working to "improve our downtown and roadways, tear down derelict housing, working with regional developers to encourage new housing here in the community." The competition for developers' dollars is stiff, LaFlamme adds.

The global pandemic in 2020 also affected how Berlin gets things done, according to LaFlamme. She says, "The pandemic really disrupted supply

The autumn River Fire event shows a united Berlin looking toward the future. *Androscoggin Valley Chamber of Commerce.*

27

chains and the national economy and has made things extremely limited like materials, contractors and workers." But Berlin is still "moving forward," she adds, "and working around what we can, where we can."

LaFlamme points to the Riverwalk along the Androscoggin as an example of a successful project. A local housing development group is retrofitting a former elementary school into twenty units of housing. And the tourism thrust continues, with the State of New Hampshire planning to double the size of the Jericho Mountain State Park campground.

"Despite the challenges we face, which aren't unique to Berlin, we are still making progress and moving forward," LaFlamme concludes.

Morneau's efforts have included helping Berlin recover its pride. He was instrumental in starting the Berlin Historical Society in 1990. "We now have a heightened awareness of Berlin history and pride," he says. Community festivals include the River Fire event every October.

"We may never get a major industry back, but we have tourism," Morneau muses.

The corrections industry has also found a welcome in Berlin. The 750-bed Northern New Hampshire Correctional Facility, built in 1999, employs 200 people. Another institution operated by the Federal Bureau of Prisons employs 350, with 1,200 beds.[6]

"We're not just a mill town," Morneau says. "We're about the resilience of the people."

And hardy New Englanders will always find a home there.

Chapter 2

BETHLEHEM

EVERYONE WELCOME HERE

For the young David Goldstone, summer meant fleeing the heat and noise of a Brooklyn neighborhood to the New Hampshire White Mountains. The small town of Bethlehem was their vacation destination. Goldstone participated in a day camp for Jewish children called Stonecrest after the bungalow colony where it was based. While the Town of Bethlehem shared its municipal golf course and swimming pool with the summer residents, there were limits, according to Goldstone. "The townies would always know when the bus from the bungalow was coming," he recalls. "Someone would yell, 'Here comes Stonecrest!' and everybody would get out of the pool."

Times changed, and Bethlehem changed with them. When Goldstone retired from his career as a landscape architect with the City of New York, he could think of no better place to call home. He's now president of the Bethlehem Hebrew Congregation and a "lifer" who doesn't mind shoveling snow, even in November.

How do a people hounded from country to country find a home in a tiny New Hampshire mountain town, with people who say *ayuh* and wear flannel?

It wasn't easy, but Goldstone and his fellow Jewish residents now say it was worth it.

Little Bethlehem has a lot going for it, besides its famous name. It is home to the Cushman and Strawberry Hill state forests, has part of its eastern portion within the White Mountain National Forest and is crossed to the

Above: The tiny village of Bethlehem (shown here at the turn of the century, 1900–1905), has been a resort town for decades. *Library of Congress, Prints & Photographs Division, FSA/OWI Collection LC-D4-500094 [P&P].*

Opposite, top: Children enjoy a basketball game at Camp Na Ha Ra, one of the Jewish hay fever relief summer camps in Bethlehem. *Bethlehem Historical Society.*

Opposite, bottom: An early view of the Herrman family's Sinclair Hotel, circa 1907. *Library of Congress, Prints & Photographs Division, FSA/OWI Collection LC-D4-19817 [P&P].*

south by the Appalachian Trail.[7] Like those of its bigger neighbor Berlin, its residents, 826 at the 2000 census, have always welcomed diversity. But there were growing pains.

Bethlehem was granted in 1774 as Lloyd's Mills by Royal Governor John Wentworth, who did a lot of granting in those days. It was named for James Lloyd of Boston. In the chaos of the Revolution, this grant was also not settled until after the war, when a few hardy families put their hands to homesteads in 1787. The town was incorporated as Bethlehem in December 1799, with thirty-three families, mostly farmers.

The railroad arrived in 1867, and the quiet mountain town changed forever, at least in the summer. Wealthy families came from New York

City to escape the steaming summer heat. The town's low pollen count, apocryphally the lowest in New Hampshire, attracted asthma sufferers.

Eventually, seven trains would arrive daily to one of Bethlehem's five railroad depots, bringing everyone from the F.W. Woolworth family to Presidents Grant, Hayes, Roosevelt, Taft and Harding (not all at the same time). Visitors stayed in hotels or built lavish summer "cottages" on the back roads. A two-and-a-half-mile boardwalk provided games and entertainment.[8]

The rise of the automobile brought an end to the "grand hotel" era. But Bethlehem was ready to welcome another set of visitors: members of New York's Jewish community. They came in waves to escape the city heat and the summer pollen. They even formed a Hebrew Hay Fever Relief Association. They stayed at the old wooden Arlington Hotel, and other hotels sprang up to accommodate them.

Ruth Pactor's mother suffered from severe asthma, and her doctor advised her to go to the White Mountains. When Mrs. Pactor protested that she couldn't afford the trip, the doctor told her, "You should go even if you have to walk." The family scraped the funds together, and Mrs. Pactor went to Bethlehem in the summer of 1924. She took a room in a rooming house owned by taxi driver/landlord Max Glantz, himself a former hay fever sufferer.[9]

Before Bethlehem, "my mother was in her early 30's but bent over she looked like a woman of 75. We couldn't believe the improvement when we came to visit her," Pactor writes. The Pactors scraped up money again, this time for their own cottage, and Mrs. Pactor was soon spending her summers "painting, wallpapering, cooking and baking," according to her daughter.[10]

The Bethlehem Heritage Website notes that the first recorded mention of the growing Jewish community was the pooling of funds to buy their own Torah, or biblical scroll. They stayed in the venerable Arlington Hotel, rooming houses or cottages. Another early recorded presence is in 1910, when Isidor and Sadie Lusher bought the Altamonte Hotel. By 1923, five hotels catered to the Jewish clients, and by 1956, there were over a dozen, including the Sinclair, the Maplewood, the Perry House, Park View, Alpine, Strawberry Hill and the Howard House.[11]

The Sons of Abraham found a second home in the mountains. In the late 1920s, they bought the former Protestant Episcopal church and established a home for the Bethlehem Hebrew congregation. In 1938, a group of women formed the Sisterhood of the Bethlehem Hebrew Congregation and began to raise money for worthy causes.

But they never lost sight of their original reason for coming. In 1919, the Jewish population of Bethlehem instituted the Hebrew Hay Fever Relief Association, and in the 1950s, the name of the group was changed to the National Hay Fever Relief Association. A summer camp for Jewish children ran on Route 142 until the 1980s.

In an article by Sarah Masor, a former executive director of the National Hay Fever Relief Association, she explained that the efforts to understand hay fever were furthered by a Dr. Herman Blum, who died in 1973. Bloom, research director of the association, used his skills to establish pollen count stations throughout the White Mountains, beginning with one at the institute. Other progress made by the institute includes several new buildings, a water drainage system, two artesian wells, a recreation hall and a camp for underprivileged children with allergies.[12]

The Goldstones started coming up to Bethlehem from Brooklyn in 1957. They stayed at the Stonecrest bungalow colony for the next fifteen years, and David got summer work at the Sinclair Hotel. He remembers the Bethlehem

New Hampshire Governor Lane Dwinell visits the Sinclair Hotel in Bethlehem. *From left*: Marty Leondar, Pauline Leondar, co-owner Dorothy Herrman, Dwinell, Mrs. Dwinell and co-owner Myron Herman. *Bethlehem Historical Society.*

of that time as being a kind of "Catskills North," with Catskill-type comics and other entertainment.

Some hotels still "restricted" themselves from Jews. Historian Clare Brown recalls, "In the early years, there was a lot of ambivalence. The Wallace Lodge on Route 302 had a sign in its advertising, 'Jews not welcome.'" So some of the Jewish businessmen went out and bought their own hotels.

The Jewish summer population was especially high in the 1930s and early '40s, according to Brown. And there were growing pains. Early on, Bethlehem's public golf course was restricted from Jewish players. Again, the summer residents took care of themselves. "A man named Mr. Berman went out and built his own golf course, on Mount Agassiz," Brown said.

But for the most part, the summer visitors blended in and were tolerated, even receiving visits from the governor. Brown's father owned a dairy, and her mother worked at it. "She remembers serving the summer Jewish visitors," Brown recalled. "There were no issues." The hotels attracted entertainers from the Catskills circuit, some of whom would go on to greater fame.

Linda Herrman saw the hotel industry up close: her parents owned the historic Sinclair Hotel in the 1940s and '50s. The Herrmans wintered in Miami but came up every summer to run the hotel. As a child, Herrman saw the "no Jews" signs, but they didn't impact her directly. "The grocery, the butcher, the baker didn't discriminate against us," she recalls.

But then Herrman rarely had to leave the hotel. It was more of a resort, she recalls, with its own swimming pool, kids' activities, adult classes and entertainment. She worked for her parents as a teen, and she and her sister hung out with fellow employees, college students from across the Northeast. She made friends and memories.

She also took in performances by current and rising stars, including a very young Harry Belafonte and comedians Alan King and Norm Crosby. "It was," Herrman says, "a lovely experience."

The "boom" was to end in mid-century, when antihistamines were developed and better air conditioning came to Florida. Those coming for hay fever relief had other options, according to Goldstone. Many Jewish families headed south instead of north. Some hotels went out of business.

The Herrmans put their hotel on the market in 1974. People were more mobile by then, Linda Herrman recalls, and interstate travel was easier, even for the Children of Abraham. "The older clientele was dying off, and the younger ones weren't interested," she says.

But Bethlehem was ready to welcome yet another set of guests, the Hasidic Jews. With their black clothing, forelocks and modest demeanor for

David the Great, a Houdini-type entertainer, performs an escape at the Sinclair Hotel. *Bethlehem Historical Society.*

No less than a young Zero Mostel clowns around in an appearance at a Bethlehem summer resort. *Bethlehem Historical Society.*

women, the Hasidim stood out—but they fit in, with new hotels catering to their dietary needs.

Hundreds of Hasidic Jewish families still drive north in July and August each year. Many stay at the new Arlington Hotel, where they can get fresh kosher food. They're a standard sight around the community, although, with their black clothing and brimmed hats, many unschooled visitors confuse them with the Amish, according to Goldstone.

Other Jewish families, like the Goldstones, cast their lot permanently with Bethlehem. The town now has a year-round Jewish population and a one-hundred-family Bethlehem Hebrew Congregation, presided over by Goldstone and ministered to by the Rabbi Donna Kirschbaum.

While the Jews were never turned away from Bethlehem, the townies and Children of Abraham maintained a mostly respectful distance in the twentieth century. The new millennium saw much more interplay, according to Goldstone.

The synagogue used to be traditional, with men and women in strictly defined roles. But even then, there were options. The building the BHC bought had a unique layout where men and women could sit apart, or if they wanted to, men could sit with their wives. The synagogue has since become egalitarian, with its first woman president, Moochoo Salamon, and

The Bethlehem Village Store now has a kosher section. *Kathleen Bailey.*

a female rabbi. The Bethlehem group has been Reform or Conservative for most of its existence, and under the current rabbi, it's "Reconstructionist," according to Goldstone. "That's somewhere in between."

Goldstone notes that it's impossible to quantify the number of Jewish families in Bethlehem. He knows most of the religious Jews because of the BHC, but other families are nonreligious Jews who moved north for a variety of reasons.

Linda Herrman has also come full circle. After a career in social work, she chose to move to Bethlehem permanently. She inherited a house on land carved out of the old Sinclair grounds and says, "I always wanted to live up here. I always liked this environment." She's made both Jewish and Gentile friends and has a busy retirement, working with the Bethlehem Historical Society. She says, "I am very comfortable living here."

The restored Colonial Theater is now home to a Jewish Film Festival attended by both Jews and Gentiles, where the Jews can explain their culture. A Jewish Book Club meets regularly at the local library. The Bethlehem Village Store has a kosher section, and a Jewish section of the town cemetery was established in 2006.

Though America has seen disturbing incidents of revived anti-Semitism in recent years, Goldstone muses that it's skipped Bethlehem. "We have," he says, "no incidents here."

Clare Brown agrees. She says, "Bethlehem is very tolerant. We have the year-round Jewish community, we have the Hasidim in summer, and in recent years we've welcomed the gay and lesbian community. We have both a Christmas tree and a menorah at the town hall. That should tell you something."

And anybody can go into the pool.

THE ROCKS: ONE MAN'S LEGACY

Nigel Manley is the first to admit he had never tasted maple syrup before immigrating to the United States in 1985. It was an expensive, exotic treat for most British people, he says.

But once he found his life's work, he got all the maple syrup he could eat.

Manley is the senior outreach manager for the Rocks Estate, a 1,400-acre forested parcel in Bethlehem managed by the Society for the Protection of New Hampshire Forests. He's been on the job since 1985 and has held a variety of positions, including site director.

The Rocks is the former summer home of Chicago businessman and co-founder of International Harvester John Jacob Glessner. Glessner and his family summered for many years in Bethlehem. Like the Hasidic Jews, the Glessner family sought the pure mountain air as a cure for asthma, this time for the son of the family. The family first bunked in rented quarters in Twin Mountain before deciding to purchase their own. Glessner bought the Orrin Streeter farm, consisting of buildings and one hundred acres, in 1882. He continued to buy up smaller farms until he owned two thousand acres.[13]

Glessner set about farming his land—or paying others to farm it. He had his own butter and potatoes shipped to his home in Chicago. He had his Christmas tree harvested on the property and shipped to his midwestern home. He had sheep, poultry, pigs and a dairy herd.

The founder of International Harvester could be expected to be inventive, and Glessner was. He had electricity on the farm before the rest of Bethlehem lit up. He had his own water system, and with his special machine shop, he could make any part he needed for his equipment.

He eventually built two houses on the property, according to Manley. One was the Big House, where Glessner himself lived, and the other was the

A spring view of the Rocks Estate in Bethlehem. *Anna Berry/Society for the Protection of New Hampshire Forests.*

Fall foliage makes a brilliant contrast against Christmas trees waiting to be tagged at the Rocks Estate in Bethlehem. *Society for the Protection of New Hampshire Forests.*

Ledges, occupied by his son George. The two houses were passed down through two separate branches of the family. Eventually, grandchildren Martha Batchelder and John Lee donated their portion, 1,300 acres and twenty-two buildings, to the Forest Society. The requirement was that there always be a crop in the field, and for more than thirty years, that crop has been Christmas trees, according to Manley. The houses were taken down sometime in the 1940s, but the land remains.

The society is currently restoring an 1884 barn to house its offices and an education center. "We are the society's headquarters for northern New Hampshire," Manley says. There are educational programs for children and families, senior bus tours and something going all year round. In the late winter, it's the maple harvest. "We contract with a local harvester, and we sell their syrup here," Manley notes. In summer it's the views, and in winter it's the Christmas tree operation.

About 1,600 families come to Bethlehem each year to choose a Christmas tree, Manley says. The farm does both wholesale and retail. Tree buyers come from the northern New England states and also from Massachusetts, Connecticut and even New York and New Jersey. The Rocks has an arrangement with several local hotels and B&Bs. "They

A sleigh ride is one of the amenities offered to families cutting their own Christmas trees at the Rocks Estate in Bethlehem. *Anna Berry/Society for the Protection of New Hampshire Forests.*

offer a two-day package, which includes lodging, a Christmas tree and a wreath," he says.

The first crop of trees was planted in 1989, and that means Manley has seen a number of repeat customers. "We get visitors I've seen for the past twenty-five years," he says, adding, "They've grown older. I stay the same." The visitors are drawn not only by the tree-cutting operation but also by toasting marshmallows at a fire pit, sleigh rides, kettle corn and the 360-degree views.

In addition, visitors can see native animals ranging from bear and moose to wild turkey, spotted salamanders and countless species of birds.

Manley has become something of an expert on Christmas trees, and he says even customers from the mid-Atlantic states don't have to worry: their Tannenbaum will survive the trip. "The stumps heal over within twelve hours," he says. "The water stays in. And we wrap them tightly, with string."

And in case you were wondering—yes, Bethlehem will cancel your Christmas cards.

Chapter 3

THE WHITE MOUNTAINS

THE OTHER OLD MAN—AND AN OLD WOMAN

In May 2003, New Hampshire said goodbye to its symbol of two hundred years. Ashen-faced newsreaders announced it on the morning report: the Old Man had fallen.

The Old Man of the Mountains had presided over the Franconia Notch area since recorded time. The formation, dubbed the "Great Stone Face," resembled a man and drew tourists to gawk at the craggy profile. The first written mention of the formation came in 1805, when a surveying team, Francis Whitcomb and Luke Brooks, noted the arrangement. It was also noted by no less than Daniel Webster and Nathaniel Hawthorne. But the image was also sacred to the Abenaki, who called it "Stone Face," and to the Mohawk. He was an equal-opportunity symbol.[14]

The Old Man stood 1,200 feet above Profile Lake and was 40 feet tall and 25 feet wide.

In 1945, the Old Man became the symbol of New Hampshire, on everything from keychains to magnets, T-shirts to official correspondence. He graced license plates, state route signs and the New Hampshire state quarter.

Rock formations are created when water enters cracks in the granite. The water freezes over time and expands, which shapes and cracks the rock. Fissures were discovered in the Old Man's forehead before the twentieth century and became critical in the 1920s. The crack was mended with chains. In 1957, the state legislature approved $25,000 for weatherproofing, including fast-drying cement, plastic covering, steel rods and a concrete gutter to divert runoff. But it wasn't enough, and the structure tumbled to the ground between midnight and 2:00 a.m. on May 3, 2003. Though replacements were discussed, the state eventually decided that the best way to memorialize the Old Man was to honor, not to replicate. Profiler Plaza now offers coin-operated viewing stations to see where the Old Man was.

But he wasn't the only rock face in the Whites.

The Indian Head in Lincoln depicts the face of a Native American, probably male, on the side of Mount Pemigewasset. Abenaki chief Pemigewasset used the top of the mountain as a lookout for enemies. His tribe lived in the White Mountains in the seventeenth and eighteenth centuries. Though the Abenaki lost control of the White Mountains after the French and Indian War, their names lived on in the region. The word *Pemigewasset* means "rapidly moving." It is also the name of a nearby river.[15]

In the early 1900s, a forest fire devastated the southern slope of Mount Pemigewasset. The trees burned away and the granite formations stood out, and one of them resembled a man. The profile looked like a Native man and was christened the Indian Head. Many felt it resembled Chief Pemigewasset.[16]

Indian Head measures 98 feet from chin to forehead. The mountain is 2,530 feet high.[17]

A tourist industry grew up in the Lincoln area, and the Indian Head Motel was established in 1913, working its way through cottages to a motel to a full-scale resort.

But the Chief never caught on as a symbol of the state or even the mountains. Perhaps his location hurt him, a side road in North Lincoln that isn't famous for anything else. US Route 3 in Lincoln is pretty enough, but it isn't a main highway, and it doesn't have the jaw-dropping vistas of Franconia Notch.

Carol Riley, president of the Upper Pemi Historical Society, agrees that the Indian Head just wasn't as prominent as the Old Man. "The Old Man really 'stuck out,'" she says. While the motel realized the profile's potential and capitalized on it, he never caught on with the general public as a symbol.

There's yet another profile, according to Riley. The locals call it the Watcher or the Old Woman. The Old Woman has a craggy profile similar to that of her more famous cousin. A stand of trees on top of the cliff can be loosely interpreted as hair.

Riley has a ready answer as to why the Watcher didn't make it onto postcards or keychains: she's not that easy to find. The agile can catch a

The Indian Head in Lincoln depicts the face of a Native American, probably male, on the side of Mount Pemigewasset. *Sheila Bailey.*

The Indian Head Motel in North Lincoln keeps the legacy alive. *Sheila Bailey.*

The Watcher, aka the Old Woman of the Mountains, is more elusive than the Old Man site or the Indian Head but worth a hike. *John Compton, the Happy Hiker.*

glimpse while driving north (with someone else in the driver's seat) and looking back to the right. It requires the moves of a contortionist.

Hikers prefer to view the Watcher from the south side of Profile Lake, while looking at the highest part of Eagle Cliff, a rock formation that is part of Mount Lafayette. But sometimes the Old Woman can play hard to get. Lexi Brocoum, who writes the *Hiking Up with the Pup* blog, admits to being challenged by the Old Woman trail, even after hiking all New Hampshire's four-thousand-footers.

Brocoum writes in a 2019 blog, "I thought that my experience hiking all of the 4,000 footers would have prepared me for something like this, but at a certain point I felt a little in over my head. I would only recommend this whack [a nickname for bushwhacking] to someone who has a lot of off trail experience specifically on steep slides."

Brocoum, who grew up splitting her time between Hopkinton and Sugar Hill, has hiked all over the world, but mostly on established trails. After the Old Man fell, she felt a sense of nostalgia, and she and hiking buddy Rob Cummings decided to trek in to see the Old Woman. "It was partly from a sense of nostalgia," Brocoum recalls, "and neither of us had ever been there."

In her quest for the Old Woman, Brocoum experienced loose rocks and at one point a loose boulder. She remembers Cummings shouting, "Rock! Rock! Rock!" "As I glanced up I saw a 2′x3′ boulder careening down at me from 50 feet above. I dove out of way, scurried to the side just in time to see the rock fly by my head where I had just been standing less than a second before. It only missed me by a yard or so. As I heard it plummet down the slope I dashed up the rest of the slide to safety."

It was risky business even for an experienced hiker, but at last Lexi, her dog Lucy and Rob stood in the presence of the Old Woman. Lexi writes, "At first I couldn't see her in the face of the rock, but as I started to take in my surroundings I distinguished her profile sticking out of the cliff. Suddenly there she was before us, her mighty gaze staring down at the valley below. Her face is wise and weathered, with crazy hair formed by the bushes on top of the cliff."

"We came to a landing, and there was an overlook about 100 or 200 feet away." Since Cummings is over six feet tall, "we couldn't stand there at the same time," she recalls.

Brocoum isn't a person who "sees shapes in clouds," she says, adding, "but she was very clear to me."

She and Cummings had done other hikes together, including ice climbing, and she says now, "I'm lucky and glad to have seen her. But I will never do it again without a helmet."

The hike is short—"I'll give it that," Brocoum says with a laugh—"but it's steep and rocky. It is not a beginner hike."

She agrees with Riley that the Old Woman, or the Watcher, can be seen from the road but adds, "You really need to know what you're looking for."

Though nobody built a plaza for the Chief or the Watcher, they're still available for the curious and diligent visitor.

"They just didn't get enough 'face time,'" Riley concludes with a smile.

LITTLETON: SOMETHING TO BE GLAD ABOUT

Littleton, a town of six thousand people[18] perched on the Ammonoosuc River, didn't have to reinvent itself to become a North Country hub. Everything it needed was already there—small businesses, an arts community and a piece of literary history.

Littleton was settled in 1764 with the melodic name of Cheswick (Old English for "cheese farm"). It was part of Lisbon until 1770, when it incorporated as a separate town under the name of Apthorp in honor of George Apthorp, a wealthy Boston merchant. The land later passed to a group of Apthorp's associates under the leadership of Colonel Moses Little of Newburyport, Massachusetts, and received its forever name of Littleton.[19]

THE SOUND OF MUSIC

These hills are alive with the sound of music, and some of it may be made by you. In spring, summer and fall, Main Street features colorfully decorated pianos along the sidewalk. Residents and visitors can stop to tap out a tune, and even if you're not musical, the colors and designs are a delight.

Littleton also offers a music experience in Harmony Park, along the Riverwalk. Five different musical stations allow visitors to play a variety of instruments, including chimes, drums or a xylophone-type installation. The instruments are embedded in the ground, and the park is open rain, shine or any combination.[20]

Left: Pollyanna Whittier was the heroine of Eleanor Hodgman Porter's classic novel *Pollyanna*. Her memory is kept alive in Porter's hometown of Littleton. *Veronica Francis/GoLittleton.*

Below: Harmony Park, on Littleton's Riverwalk, allows everyone to make their own kind of music. *Veronica Francis/ GoLittleton.*

According to the GoLittleton website, Dave Ernsberger, owner of the Nest art gallery, saw a similar setup in a community park in Sedona, Arizona. He said, "Everyone was enjoying making music together with these unique instruments. And since we already had pianos located throughout town that residents and tourists have enjoyed over the years, I thought this would be a great addition to making the town even more musical—especially along the River District where people are always out walking." So Ernsberger did his homework and discovered that Freenotes Harmony Park, a Colorado company, was the best choice for the instruments. John Starr helped design the park, and Ron Bolt oversaw the installation. The park was dedicated and opened on the second Saturday in June 2015 as part of the town's Glad Day (see below).

The park is part of the River District, which winds along the Ammonoosuc River behind Main Street, from the multi-modal bridge on Bridge Street through the Apthorp District on Union Street and beyond into Bethlehem via the Rail Trail. In addition to Harmony Park, the River District includes multiple footbridges, a walking path, restaurants and more.

The visual arts have a vibrant presence in Littleton, from murals on Main Street buildings to a League of New Hampshire Craftsmen shop to the Littleton Studio School. Live theater can be seen in the Littleton Opera House, and live music can be heard in various venues around town.

BRING YOUR CREDIT CARD

Chutters, a local candy and souvenir shop, has the longest candy counter in the world.[21]

Try the Little Village Toy and Book Shop for a curated collection of toys, books and souvenirs.

The White Mountain Canning Company presents jams and jellies, pickles and other preserved items and more, with a local focus.

Other shops, both on Main Street and along the River Walk, offer antiques and boutique items.

LIVE WITH A LEGEND

But the ribbon that ties it all together is a slip of a girl invented by an author just after the turn of the twentieth century.

Chutters, Littleton's premier candy store, has the longest candy counter in the world. It's in the *Guinness Book of World Records*. *Kathleen Bailey.*

Eleanor Hodgman Porter (1868–1920) lived in Littleton as a child. Her most famous creation, the little girl Pollyanna, first enchanted readers in 1913 and later charmed audiences in the Walt Disney film starring Hayley Mills.

Who was Pollyanna? In the novel, she is the daughter of missionaries, sent home to a small American town after her parents died. She is sent to live with her Aunt Polly, a strict, rich and tightfisted young woman who doesn't want to be bothered with a child. Pollyanna believes there's always something to be glad about, a fact that first mystifies the dour townspeople. But she continues to bring the light, and the residents begin to thaw out. After a serious accident, the town rallies around the little girl who changed them, and they wait to welcome her back home.

A bronze statue of Littleton's most famous fictional resident stands on the library lawn. It's difficult to resist the little girl flinging her arms wide in pure joy.[22]

She was difficult for Veronica Francis to resist. Though Pollyanna had always been a part of Littleton, the construction of the statue by the late Emile Birch, funded by the Eames family, brought her front and center. "People came out of the woodwork" to acknowledge Littleton's most famous

The Hodgman home in Littleton. *Littleton Historical Society.*

resident and her creation, and Francis knew the interest had to be nourished. She opened her GoLittleton website to promote what's good about the town, and in 2019, she opened the Glad Shop to further explain the phenomenon. The Glad Shop at 91 Main Street is a source for Pollyanna- and Littleton-related mementoes. Those interested can sign up for a Glad Club and receive periodic inspirational memos.

Pollyanna has since become the symbol for all things good in Littleton and the linchpin for GoLittleton, a civic boosters' organization headed by Francis. The group celebrates Glad Day on the second Saturday in June, with selfies, cake on the library lawn, seminars on Porter's work and more. The program has grown even further since the COVID-19 pandemic, according to Francis, who says simply, "We need it."

In 2019, a group of residents went to Concord, where Governor Chris Sununu signed a proclamation establishing the second Saturday in June as Glad Day. Glad Day welcomes people from all over the state, the region and the world. More than one hundred attended the 2023 event, according to Francis.

The celebration is complete with Littleton's own Eleanor, Historical Society member Debbie Alberini, who dresses up as the author and does her own one-woman show.

The attendees have come to know Pollyanna through different means, according to Francis. Many of the older guests remember the 1960 Disney film, which introduced actress Hayley Mills to American audiences. Others stumbled on the book or had a treasured family copy.

The group also celebrates Porter's birthday in December, but that's a little quieter, Francis says. "We have a tea party."

The Glad Club is a revival of a phenomenon from the 1920s, Francis says. "They were all over in the '20s, in our country and Europe." The clubs died out in the '30s and '40s but have slowly been revived, at least by Francis. "We have over three hundred members," she notes.

In her shop, she sells all kinds of Pollyanna and positive-thinking material, including puzzles, ornaments, dish towels and teacups. She also sells copies of the original *Pollyanna*, the book that started it all, and staff members will gladly stamp the book with a "Glad Town" stamp.

Porter wrote other books, including *Pollyanna Grows Up*, and many hit the bestseller list of her time. Her most famous work went through forty-seven printings by 1920 and was made into a Broadway play, in addition to the Disney film in 1960 and a 1920 silent movie starring Mary Pickford.

Porter was vocally gifted, performing around the area and studying at the New England Conservatory of Music in Boston. She married businessman

Eleanor Hodgman Porter at the 1916 Old Home Day celebration. *Littleton Historical Society.*

John Lyman Porter in 1892 and became a permanent resident of Massachusetts. But she often came home to Littleton, including a platform appearance in the 1916 Old Home Day. She was the only woman on a platform filled with male dignitaries.

But her greatest accomplishment, at least in Littleton's eyes, is the story of a lonely little girl who changed a community. Francis remembers one Glad Day guest who came all the way from Australia. "She had all the books, and they meant a lot to her," Francis says. "She lost her parents when she was extremely young."

Richard Alberini, curator of the Littleton Historical Society, says that Hodgman and her most famous creation weren't a big deal for Littleton during the twentieth century. The push to recognize the town's most famous daughter started around 2002. "People had no idea," Richard says, "that Pollyanna was connected with Littleton."

One resident, Linda McShane, made it her mission to bring the little girl and her creator to the forefront. McShane had written several books on Littleton history, discovered the connection and promoted it. "She brought Pollyanna into the light," Alberini muses.

Richard's wife, Debbie, portrays Eleanor Porter in civic functions and at Glad Day. "Interestingly enough, the people who come here to hear about Eleanor aren't usually from Littleton or even New Hampshire," she says. The curious are mostly tourists, and Debbie has clocked thirty-one states and eighteen countries.

She and Richard "always dressed up" for Glad Day, usually in Victorian garb, and it wasn't long before she was asked to portray Porter. She shares her research on Glad Day; Porter's birthday, December 19; in March for Women in History Month; and at churches and civic events. Debbie has done her homework but admits, "There's not a lot out there. There's a little bit here, a little bit there."

Porter didn't start writing until after she married, Debbie notes. Her husband traveled, and she was frequently alone in their Cambridge house. She published two hundred short stories and fifteen novels. She died in 1920 at the age of fifty-one.

What was Porter like beyond the typewriter? "From what I've learned, I think she was the original Pollyanna," Debbie muses. She tries to bring that light to her presentations. She's an optimist herself and says, "Maybe that's why I was asked to play her."

"Good, I'll get you a pair of crutches for Christmas," Richard cracks.

Debbie especially enjoys marching in parades as Porter. "I have so much fun," she says. "I look at the little girls, give them stickers, bookmarks." She tries to connect with the children and pass on Porter's message, especially to girls, to help them see their potential.

The Littleton Historical Museum doesn't have a lot of information on its most famous resident, according to Richard. There are a couple of photos, including the 1916 Old Home Day, her portrait and a Christmas card signed by Porter. But her Littleton roots run deep, Richard adds, and there's a lot of material on her grandfather Francis Hodgman, a jeweler and pharmacist.

Though the name "Pollyanna" made it into the dictionary as a euphemism for sometimes blind optimism, Porter insisted that her original intent wasn't cluelessness. Quoted on the GoLittleton website, Porter said, "Pollyanna did not pretend that everything was sugar-coated goodness. Instead, Pollyanna was positively determined to find the good in every situation."[23]

Pollyanna, that most American of children, even has a presence in Brazil and Turkey, where the stories are "required reading" in some curriculum. "Turkey's a place where they need some optimism," Francis muses, adding, "But it's tricky. There's no specific word for 'glad' in Turkish."

Richard Alberini agrees. "She's a big thing in Japan, Brazil. Eleven years ago, we had a journalist from Tokyo visit Littleton. I opened the museum for her, and it was as if she'd found the Holy Grail."

Chapter 4

THE LAKES REGION

THE LUCKNOW ESTATE (CASTLE IN THE CLOUDS)

Thomas Plant pulled himself up by his own bootstraps—and made his fortune selling those boots to others.

Thomas Gustave Plant was born in 1859 in Bath, Maine, to French Canadian parents of limited means. He left school at fourteen to help support the family. After a series of jobs, he took a position as a shoe laster in a footwear factory.

That's where it gets interesting.

Plant rose from laborer to owner in a little more than a decade. At thirty-two, he established the Thomas G. Plant Company. By 1910, his Jamaica Plain, Massachusetts factory was the largest factory in the United States and the largest shoe factory in the world.

While Charles Clark, director of the Lucknow Estate, is still researching much of Plant's beliefs, he pinpoints Plant's business philosophy as something called "welfare capitalism." "It means if you take care of your workers, they will work harder for you," he explains. Plant's factory complex included an on-site barber, on-site childcare and other amenities.

Clark explains, "If you never have to leave the factory, you can produce more shoes."

Welfare capitalism did well by Plant. He sold the business in 1910. Only fifty-one and wealthy, he began to plan his retirement. In 1910, he met Olive Dewey on a trip through Europe. Dewey came from a well-fixed midwestern family who sent her to Wellesley College. Higher education for women was

Thomas Plant, on horseback, surveys his estate. *Charles Clark/Castle in the Clouds.*

still a rarity in those times, according to Clark. She studied Latin and Greek and taught school.

Plant divorced his first wife around the time of his retirement. Though Olive was more than twenty years his junior, they matched each other in ambition and the ability to spend and were married in the spring of 1913.

Plant already knew where he wanted his dream house—high on the side of Mount Ossipee in Moultonborough, in New Hampshire's Lakes Region. One of his brothers lived in Tuftonboro, and the retired shoe magnate was familiar with the area.

But the area had never seen anything like the Plants or anything like their mountainside home. He and Olive designed a stunning Arts and Crafts mansion with sixteen rooms, a stable for their horses, a garage for the motorcars gaining in popularity, tennis and golf amenities, a greenhouse, a man-made lake plus a boathouse with frontage on Lake Winnipesaukee.

"The appeal," Clark says, "was apparent."

Plant began to buy up the small farms in the area. In his New Hampshire business dealings, Clark characterizes him as "not ruthless, exactly, but aggressive."

As he relaxes in the comfortable stone Admin Building, Clark elaborates. "One family had a homestead near what's now known as Shannon Pond.

Tom purchased all the land around them, but these people refused to sell. So Tom had his workers erect a 'spite fence.'" The spite fence blocked the holdouts' view of the lake, and it was built "as ugly as possible," according to Clark. That just lasted until the beleaguered family finally decided to sell. Then Plant had the fence rebuilt in a much more appealing aesthetic.

But he was also generous, as long as his own interests weren't threatened. He endowed a retirement home for the working poor in his hometown of Bath, Maine, "and it's still there," according to Clark.

Olive Dewey married shoe magnate Thomas Plant and joined him in a life of luxury. *Charles Clark/Castle in the Clouds.*

The house was designed to blend in with the rural setting. The builders used local materials such as Maine white oak and Conway pink granite for the stone veneer.

Olive had little input in the building but chose the furniture, drapes and rugs. She made the greenhouse and gardens her project.

Plant's dream house had all the modern conveniences of the time, including central vacuum, refrigeration and a house-wide phone system. But it was also a perfect fulfillment of the Arts and Crafts vision, designed to blend in with the landscape and made, whenever possible, with local materials.

The Plants also added amenities to the outside, including riding stables, golf and tennis courts and hiking trails. Fishing was available. There were forty miles of trails for riding, carriage driving or hiking. In inclement weather, there was a full library for reading or board games.

Like all the rooms, the library has floor-to-ceiling windows looking out at the lakes and mountains. Bookshelves line the room. The silk wallcoverings were replicated in 2003, part of an effort to restore as much of the castle to its former appearance as possible. The walls are lined with sculptures and paintings, including a Belgian tapestry, from the Plants' European trips. There's a pool table and a gramophone—and even a pipe organ. The multitalented Olive played the organ, made by the Aeolian Company.

The upstairs holds a large primary bedroom, Olive's dressing room, a sewing room and several good-sized guest rooms. Bathrooms are spacious and modern.

An early view of the Lucknow Mansion and greenhouse. *Charles Clark/Castle in the Clouds.*

The Lucknow Mansion. *Charles Clark/Castle in the Clouds.*

Olive Dewey Plant enjoyed canoeing on the lake at the Lucknow Estate, later to be known as the Castle in the Clouds. *Charles Clark/Castle in the Clouds.*

There's plenty of room for guests, and the Plants often entertained, though no records survive of famous visitors. "Most of the stories have been disproven," Clark says, including one with the Plants putting up Teddy Roosevelt. "There are meticulous records of where Teddy stayed, and he never made it north of Manchester," Clark says.

The people who did visit, he adds, came for weeks and, in some cases, months. Getting there was complicated, he says: first the train from Boston, then a boat ride across the lake, then a wagon ride up the mountain.

Back on the first floor, a dining room is set for four with crystal glasses and gold-rimmed china. The servants' dining room is more basic, with a cupboard holding white caps and aprons and a narrow back stairway.

THE EARL OF OSSIPEE

The refrigeration system ran on ammonia and brine, far superior to the iceboxes of the day, according to Clark. Electricity was provided by a generator, seven years before Moultonborough got electricity. Though Plant provided jobs and did business in the community, Clark speculates that there may have been "some resentment" from his poorer neighbors. He amplifies: "Imagine looking up the mountain and seeing the 'castle' lit up, when you're using candles or gas lamps." Resentment lingered most in the families who had been displaced from the mountain, and Clark muses that some express resentment to this day.

Local newspapers satirized Plant as "the earl of Ossipee Park," Clark adds.

The mansion was also built with forward-thinking construction techniques, according to Clark. Plant demanded the industrial building techniques of his time, including steel beams and poured concrete, rather than the typical home-building techniques. This resulted in a home that could resist strong mountain winds, New Hampshire winters, hurricanes and even fire. "Tom had a factory fire during his early years," Clark says, "and he never forgot it. There's a fire hose built into the house and attached to the water supply."

But Lucknow is above all the home of two people who enjoyed indulging themselves and each other.

Was Olive a trophy wife? Clark thinks not. "The indication," he says, "is that they were really fond of each other."

The Plants settled in and enjoyed a luxurious retirement until they couldn't anymore. Free spending and unwise investments meant that by the 1920s, the couple's finances were tight.

A GREEK TRAGEDY

Clark has also delved into the reasons for their financial decline. Some was from the Depression; some came from simply bad business decisions by Plant. His charitable instinct in opening the retirement home in Bath was sucking up funds. He invested in a golf club on Lake Winnipesaukee and never made back his stake. He invested in sugarcane futures, a volatile market, according to Clark. "And," Clark says with a rueful grin, "he invested in Russian bonds just before the Bolshevik revolution."

Clark also doesn't discount the cost of running Lucknow, with thirty to forty staffers between the house, grounds and stables.

It was a Greek tragedy for the once-happy consumers. The couple began selling off parcels of their 6,300 acres. An attempt to sell Lucknow brought no takers, though a friend took over the mortgage. The buyers allowed the Plants to stay at Lucknow until Tom's death in 1941, but the glory days were done. The estate was foreclosed upon. Olive took a few personal things and returned to her family in Illinois. She ended her days in Southern California.

The Tobey family of Plymouth bought what was left of the property and enjoyed it as a summer home until they sold it to Richard Robie in 1956. Robie had the vision for what became the Castle in the Clouds, opening the estate to the public in 1959. After Robie's death, his son Richard Robie Jr. operated the complex until 1991. As "The Castle," it became a beloved Lakes Region attraction.

The Robies didn't spend a lot of money or time on restoration, according to Clark. They simply operated the house as an attraction. But they kept the idea alive until a nonprofit group stepped in, and up, to preserve the Plants' legacy.

YOU *CAN* DRINK THE WATER

A group called the Castle Acquisition Partnership purchased the estate in 1991. While they had plans for expansion, their real focus was the spring water on the property. They developed and sold Castle Springs bottled water. Their other commercial entity was a brewery, and they ran the Castle concurrently with the businesses for several years.

In 2002, the Lakes Region Conservation Trust (LRCT) raised $5.9 million, through a grassroots effort, to purchase the remainder of the original Lucknow estate, 5,500 acres. The nonprofit Castle Preservation

Society (CPS) was formed to look after the house and immediate grounds, and LRCT continues to manage the other land.

Since 2006, CPS has been responsible for the restoring and preserving of the Plants' legacy. The nonprofit has added a restaurant, trout pond, café, live music and hiking trails.

The CPS has invested $5 million, so far, in restoration, according to Clark. But they're determined that the house be maintained as a house. "We have minimal areas that are roped off," he explains. "We want to give visitors an immersive experience that they can do at their own pace." There are books on the bedside tables, beaded 1920s dresses hanging from pegs, tables set for meals or afternoon tea.

The property was added to the National Register of Historic Places in 2018.

These and other historic homes give a glimpse into the way people lived—in the 603 way. These are not the Newport mansions. Whatever "excess" is reasonable. Who wouldn't want a central vacuum and a refrigerator, especially in 1914?

"It's sixty years of history," Clark says. "I often hear people say, 'I came here as a child. Now I'm coming back with my grandchildren.'"

LOOKING FORWARD

Clark hopes the estate will be around for another sixty years, and another sixty after that. The buildings have been saved through the CPS and their own excellent construction. The CPS is working on interior restoration, one room at a time, until they reflect the Plants' vision and lives.

Their strategic plan includes "turning our attention to how we can better make this a resource for the community," Clark says. Part of that will be partnering with other agencies. Lucknow already hosts the Great Waters Music Festival for several performances in the summer. They host a story time by the Moultonborough Public Library, drawing up to twenty-five children per week. They work with the Conservation Trust to make sure the grounds are accessible. "They have thirty-five miles of hiking trails, and we have bathrooms and other amenities," he notes.

And they'll continue to execute the vision of the man he calls simply "Tom." Asked how Tom would react to the modern world, Clark says that Plant would have embraced technology. "He was always into the most cutting-edge technology of his time," Clark says. "He invented better shoe-making equipment for his factories." Clark references the refrigeration and electricity at Lucknow and concludes, "Today the house would be off the grid. Tom would have solar power, hydroelectric capabilities."

LACONIA: A TOWN FOR ALL SEASONS

Before we go any further, let's dispel the idea of there being a "one and only" Laconia. Laconia is the city itself, bustling with shops, businesses and a classic downtown, including the Belknap County courthouse. Laconia is the sophisticated condos along Paugus Bay and small heirloom camps lining the shore. And Laconia is Weirs Beach, a colorful patchwork of memories, motorcycles and mayhem.

Long before Europeans discovered the potential surrounding the Big Lake, the Indigenous people were already there. One of the region's largest settlements was Acquadocton Village, in the spot now known as the Weirs and Weirs Beach. The canny Natives set woven wooden fishing baskets across the waterway. The contraptions, known as weirs, eventually gave the area its name.

Europeans were slow to discover the Weirs and slower to settle. Though the Endicott party visited the shores in 1652, now commemorated by Endicott Rock, they didn't return until 1727. They were distracted by a little thing called the French and Indian War. But return they did, with the town of Gilmanton chartered in 1727 and a fort built in the current Laconia in 1746. Europeans didn't settle for good until 1761, in a village called Meredith Bridge that is now part of downtown Laconia.

BELKNAP MILL: THE JOY OF SOCKS

While Laconia started out as a farming community, the presence of the Winnipesaukee River groomed the area for the Industrial Revolution. The Bean Carding Mill opened its doors in 1800; the Avery Mill, in 1813. The town became a center for the manufacture of trolley cars with the C. Ranlet Car Manufacturing Company, which moved to town in 1848. There were sawmills, cotton mills and companies that manufactured industrial knitting equipment.

Hardy French Canadians again found a place at the looms and other machines, along with workers from farther-flung climes. Laconia flourished as a manufacturing center.

The Belknap Mill is one of Laconia's greatest treasures. Saved from a wrecking ball in the 1970s, it now hosts civic events and offers a museum of the mill years. *Kathleen Bailey.*

And the Belknap Mill was built in 1832. The structure replaced an earlier wooden mill that had burned. It borrowed much of its design from a mill in Waltham, Massachusetts, one of the first to "integrate" the process of manufacturing textiles, from raw cotton to finished cloth. The integrated model foreshadowed mass production and assembly lines, the heart of the Industrial Revolution.

It was an elegant structure even then, with its brick and post-and-beam construction, high windows, exposed beams and open floor plan. The bell that summoned employees to work was cast by George Holbrook, an apprentice to Paul Revere.

In 1861, the Belknap Mill once again led the nation's textile mills, this time in a conversion from weaving to knitting. It was a leading producer of the nation's hosiery through the Civil War and World Wars I and II. But cheaper southern labor costs and even cheaper offshore costs told the old, old story, and the mill closed in 1969.

Urban renewal showed up around the same time and slated the mill for destruction in order to build a parking lot. This didn't go down well with the good citizens of Laconia, and they formed the Save the Mill Society. Residents Peter Karagianis and Arthur Nighswander headed the group.

In those dinosaur years of historic preservation, saving mills wasn't easy. The effort initially garnered skepticism from residents who didn't see the potential of the gracious building. Save the Mill persevered, eventually raising $500,000 to save the structure. They were the first organization to receive federal funds for preserving an industrial structure, and the effort was noted in *Life* magazine, *Yankee* and the Archie comic strip.

While they were at it, they saved the neighboring Busiel Mill (1853). The Busiel Mill is now an office building.

The Belknap Mill is listed on the National Register of Historic Landmarks as the oldest unaltered brick textile mill in the United States.

The mill was to figure in Laconia history in another way, with its water-powered wheelhouse supplying electricity to the downtown area in the early 1900s. The wheelhouse is also the last of its kind in America.

The mill building now hosts a writers' group, a knitting circle, family craft days, art exhibits and groups such as Laconia Rotary. It's a living, working entity, not a dusty relic. But it's also a museum, affording visitors a glance into

Laconia's Busiel Mill was saved by early historic preservationists and now adds charm to downtown as an office building. *Kathleen Bailey.*

Above: Weirs Beach is home to the Veterans Association compound, originally built after the Civil War. *Sheila Bailey.*

Left: The iconic Weirs Beach sign has promised fun to generations of lakeside visitors. *Kathleen Bailey.*

the building's storied past. There are three permanent exhibits: the Hosiery Museum, focusing on the production of socks; the Powerhouse Museum, focusing on early hydroelectric power; and the Mill itself.

In 1840, Belknap County was formed, and the town's courthouse, another early classic, was designated as the county court.

Meanwhile, Laconia was evolving into a vacation hub for weary Victorians. Wealthy city dwellers took the train and then the trolley to dip their toes in the Big Lake or watch it from verandas. In 1875, the New Hampshire Veterans Association formed to provide respite for Civil War veterans and was responsible for building a compound of stately Queen Anne houses. Some were destroyed by attrition and some by a lightning fire in 1931, but others survive to this day. The remaining buildings are listed on the National Register of Historic Places.

As Hampton Beach is the raucous playground for New Hampshire's eighteen miles of coast, Weirs Beach is the playground for the Lakes Region. It's the place to get your fried dough or your fried anything. It's arcades and blaring music and T-shirt shops, a carnival atmosphere that swaggers its way through late spring, summer and early fall. It's the kind of place where you are loath to drop off your tween daughter to fend for herself, because she'll probably do the same things you did when you were a tween daughter.

But Weirs Beach has become more family-friendly over the years, and so has its signature event, Motorcycle Week.[24]

THE MUSIC MEN

Laconia knows how to hang on to treasured old buildings, and not all of them are mills. In 1890, the village of Lakeport was part of Gilford. A group of citizens got together to form the Lakeport Library in rented quarters. Soon after Laconia annexed the village in 1893, the library collection went with it. Though a system for exchanging books ran out of a local store, Lakeport no longer had a physical library of its own. But a bequest from Dr. Ossian Wilbur Goss provided $7,262 for "furnishing, equipping and maintaining suitable Reading Parlors for the use and enjoyment of the general public of Lakeport." Goss originally intended the building for his home, to become a library after his death. But he died in 1903, at the age of forty-seven, from Bright's disease. His wife and heirs predeceased him. So trustees went ahead with the building plan.

The Reading Room was built on Goss land. Goss's father, also a physician, had lived there, and Ossian moved in when he began his practice. But the house, and most of Lakeport, was lost in the Great Lakeport Fire of 1903. Goss had intended to rebuild and donate the building as a library after his death, but he didn't live long enough.

The Reading Room was dedicated in 1908. Designed by Boston architect Willard P. Adden, the library maintains a simple elegance. The single-story building is covered by a gabled roof, with caps at the end. A front-facing gable window is to the right, with a large six-part window in segmented arch openings. The library has narrow windows on the outside, a wider one in the center and fixed transoms. The entry vestibule is flanked by corner brick piers and double-wide sidelights.

The Reading Room was added to the National Register of Historic Buildings in 1986 and honored on its 100th anniversary by the Lakeport Community Association in May 2008.

The Reading Room survived a 2010 challenge to close it. While the library trustees brought the proposal forward to fill a $20,000 shortfall, city councilors pointed to the historical and cultural significance of the building. But it never reopened after the 2020 pandemic and is still awaiting its next use.

Laconia is a place where the unexpected can happen. When Recycled Percussion, a nationally known percussion band with New Hampshire roots, wanted to set up a store for its merch, the members chose Lakeport. The band members, including leader Justin Spencer, didn't expect to find anything beyond a brick-and-mortar store for their stuff.

But an elderly man with a disability wandered in off the street and helped himself to the free candy, taking more than his share. His name was Roy Small. Small was a musician who traversed the country as a Roy Orbison impersonator. (Yes, that's a thing.) A stroke sidelined him, affecting his ability to speak, and he returned to Laconia, eventually moving in with his daughter Karen Houle.

When staff members brought the candy conundrum to Spencer, he determined to handle it himself. But when he confronted Roy Small, both men's lives changed.[25]

The band helped Small in big and little ways. They purchased guitars and equipment for him. They invited him to play in their local concerts, including a bring-the-house-down version of Orbison's "Any Way You Want." They had him on their television show, *Chaos and Kindness*, and supported him in any way they could until his death.[26]

Recycled Percussion's adoption of Small is a particularly New Hampshire phenomenon. Spencer could have just sent him back to his daughter with a stern warning or bought him his own bag of taffy. The band could have given him food, clothes or money. But in a spirit that transcends charity, they treated him like they would have wanted to be treated. They got him back on stage. And when he died, they memorialized him with a bench outside their Lakeport store.[27]

It's an attitude that thrives in the 603. We don't want to see anything go to waste, whether it's an old mill or a musician.

Chapter 5

THE UPPER VALLEY

SUMMER HOMES: BEYOND THE VERANDA

New Hampshire has long been a summertime destination, from the Orthodox Jews who fled Manhattan's heat to rest and recreate in Bethlehem, to Senator Mitt Romney and his hideaway on the Big Lake. Sometimes a "summer home" is renting the same cottage every year or owning a semi-shack with questionable plumbing, but that doesn't matter because you're In the Woods or On the Lake. And sometimes the summer cottage takes on a life of its own. We look at two summer homes that have become beloved parts of the New Hampshire landscape, years after their owners left this earth.

THE FELLS

Simon Parsons, former education director for The Fells, loves to tell a story about when President Theodore Roosevelt stayed overnight at the estate. "Teddy said he didn't sleep all night because the dog was barking," Parsons says, adding, "The dog's name was Boxer."

The Fells in Newbury is the summer home of diplomat John Hay, restored and preserved, along with extensive gardens, for the enjoyment and enrichment of generations to come. It was a private home, albeit an elegant one, and the perfect place for a busy diplomat to refresh his spirits—even if his dog kept his commander-in-chief awake.

The Fells in Newbury was the summer home of diplomat John Hay. *Sheila Bailey.*

At only twenty-two, John Hay was tapped to be Abraham Lincoln's private secretary. He later served as secretary of state under Presidents William McKinley and Theodore Roosevelt.

Born in 1838, Hay was the son of an Illinois country doctor. He graduated from Brown University, where he was also known as the "class poet," according to a video shown by the estate. He returned to Illinois and became friends with one Abraham Lincoln. When Lincoln won the presidential election, Hay accompanied him to Washington as one of two personal secretaries.[28]

It was the beginning of a career in government that would span forty years. Hay was there for Lincoln during the War Between the States, and he sat at his commander-in-chief's bedside on that fateful night in April 1865.

Hay married Clara Louise Stone in 1875 and continued his career in politics, serving in diplomatic posts in Paris, Vienna and Madrid. The couple became friends with author Henry Adams and his wife, Clover, and with Clarence King, an explorer and geologist, and his wife. Looking for a refuge from city life and the rough-and-tumble world of politics, the three couples made plans to find adjacent rural retreats. Clover Adams's untimely death halted their plans. Augustus Saint-Gaudens memorialized her death with a statue now at the Saint-Gaudens Historic Site.

With King's help, the couple found a tract of land in rural Newbury, New Hampshire. John Hay bought up neighboring farms at twenty-five cents an acre, eventually accumulating one thousand acres. He named his place The Fells, a British term for a rocky upland pasture and a tribute to his Scottish ancestry.

Architect George F. Hammond designed the Colonial Revival, gambrel-roofed house. Construction was completed in 1892, with the eventual addition of another "cottage-style" house, also designed by Hammond, in 1897. A central foyer connected them both.

Diplomat John Hay as painted by John Singer Sargent. *John Hay Estate at The Fells.*

As the family arrived by boat, the main entrance faced Lake Sunapee.

Hay loved it all. He enjoyed the outdoors, and in one letter to Henry Adams, he wrote, "I am daft over the lake!"

Though the property was too rocky for the Hays to keep horses, they had other amusements including boating, hiking and, on rainy days, board games in the library.

The place was a refuge from the heat, dirt and noise of Washington—and the politics. Clara Hay gardened, growing roses and hydrangeas. They entertained prolifically, with guests from the cultural, political and entertainment worlds including sculptor Augustus Saint-Gaudens and Rudyard Kipling.

And one president.

Teddy Roosevelt signed the guest book in 1902. Hay had been appointed secretary of state under President William McKinley. When McKinley was assassinated in September 1901, Roosevelt ascended to the presidency, and Hay worked under him. The house now has a "Teddy room," with a derby, walking stick and other memorabilia.

The property was still relatively primitive during the Hays' lifetime. Ice-age boulders littered the property, and sheep grazed nearby. Another generation would make the farm hideaway an estate.

Hay continued to work in diplomacy. He helped shape Roosevelt's foreign policy, negotiated the treaty for the Panama Canal, promoted the Open

President Theodore Roosevelt visited the Hays in August 1902. He is shown here at Newbury Harbor. Hay is on his right, with George Cotelyou, cabinet secretary, to the left. *John Hay Estate at The Fells.*

Door policy with China and mediated the Alaska border dispute. In his last year, he tried to broker a peace agreement between China and Japan.

John Hay died at The Fells in 1905. His son Clarence inherited the property, and with his wife, Alice Appleton Hay, he expanded on his parents' vision with terraced lawns and formal gardens, creating the elegant home visitors see today. Alice Appleton came from money, as they say, and her childhood home, Appleton Farms, was a showplace. According to Parsons, she "burst into tears" when she first saw the home her husband had inherited.

But Clarence's soul was linked to Alice's, at least where style was concerned. Two of his Harvard classes resonated with him the rest of his life, one on forestry and one on landscaping taught by the renowned Frederick Law Olmsted.

Local architect Prentice Sanger shared their vision and helped reshape the cottages into the Colonial Revival style. Sanger remodeled the passageway between the houses into a full connecting building. Alice Hay modeled the gardens on ones she had seen in Italy and France. She particularly loved working with roses.

Above: Alice Appleton Hay stands in the rose garden she lovingly restored at The Fells in Newbury, the summer home of generations of the Hay family. *John Hay Estate at The Fells.*

Opposite, top: The library at The Fells. *Kathleen Bailey.*

Opposite, bottom: One of the extensive gardens at The Fells in Newbury, the summer home of diplomat John Hay. *Sheila Bailey.*

The house served as a summer home for three generations of the Hay family. Clarence and Alice were in residence June through September, spending the fall and winter in New York.

The house has been restored and maintains many of the original features, including Persian carpets and glass doorknobs. A large and comfortable library looks out over the gardens, with floor-to-ceiling windows letting in the light. Most of the books on the shelves are original to the Hay family, with only the rarest volumes given over to the Brown University library.

The dining room can accommodate eight but probably accommodated more with extensions. The gleaming table sits on an Oriental rug. A pedimented fireplace and crown moldings add elegance. It's easy to imagine sparkling dinner conversation from the many notables who stayed over.

The bedrooms upstairs are comfortable and classic without being ostentatious. There's a "box room" for suitcases, with an ironing board so no one looked rumpled after their travels. The bathrooms are modern, for 1902,

The porch at The Fells in Newbury is a perfect spot for afternoon tea on the veranda. *Sheila Bailey.*

with flush toilets and running water. There's a room for young travelers to stay over, with toys and games and a dollhouse. And in an age when women wore hats, there's a closet devoted entirely to hatboxes. Each room has a call bell for servants. Alice brought her own staff but in the summer entertaining season also hired local women, usually college students.

The property consists of the home, the gardens and the John Hay National Wildlife Refuge. Conservation was always a consideration. In 1960, the surviving Hays donated 675 acres to the Society for the Protection of New Hampshire Forests. After Clarence Hay died in 1969, his wife, Alice, donated 164 acres to the United States Fish and Wildlife Service. She reserved 143 acres for the use of herself and her survivors. After her death in 1987, the remaining land became the John Hay National Wildlife Refuge.

The refuge now comprises eighty acres and includes hardwood trees, softwood trees, a brook, a meadow, vernal pools and three thousand feet of land along the shore of Lake Sunapee. There are wildflower gardens, a rock garden Clarence worked on for forty years, Alice's beloved roses and more.

A not-for-profit, The Fells, was created in 1996 to manage the house and land. The house is managed by a board of directors and staffed by paid staff and volunteers. It is listed on the National Register of Historic Places.

THE SAINT-GAUDENS NATIONAL HISTORIC SITE

Kerstin Burlingame likes to play a game with her coworkers and the guests at the Saint-Gaudens Historic Site in Cornish. The supervisory park ranger says, "We ask people to connect Saint-Gaudens with anything else you can bring up." It's not as hard as you'd think, she says cheerfully. "There's one of his Lincolns in Mexico City. There's one in Trafalgar Square, London. A relief portrait he did of Robert Louis Stevenson hangs in a chapel in Edinburgh."

"There are," she says, "usually only one or two degrees of separation."

Augustus Saint-Gaudens was a noted sculptor of his time who created more than 150 sculptures; designed the 1907 twenty-dollar gold piece, widely considered the most beautiful American coin ever cast; and founded and mentored the Cornish Colony of artists. He designed everything from cameos to full-scale sculpture installations—and left much of it in New Hampshire.

"It's not just the big monuments," Burlingame notes. "Some people come here just to see the coins."

Saint-Gaudens was born in Ireland, but his parents moved to the United States when he was six months old, and he was raised in the Bowery section of New York City. His mother was Irish and his father French, and both were cobblers. Because they had skills, they skipped the "No Irish need apply" discrimination, and young Augustus was raised in the lower middle class. He still left school in eighth grade to help support the family. Apprenticed to a cameo cutter, he found the work boring but learned discipline and detail.[29]

His father, Bernard, saved young Augustus's wages, and when Augustus was nineteen, Bernard presented him with $100. The man he was apprenticed to matched the gift, and Augustus set off for Paris to learn sculpting. It was arguably the best investment his father and his old boss ever made.

Augustus studied art in Paris during the Gilded Age. He was the first American to be

Noted sculptor Augustus Saint-Gaudens chose to make his summer home, and later his forever home, in a tiny town on the New Hampshire/Vermont border. *National Park Service/ Saint-Gaudens National Historic Site.*

enrolled in the prestigious École des Beaux-Arts. There were a number of lean years, according to Burlingame, but he survived, and his work began to attract attention. He also met his wife, the painter Augusta Homer, in Paris. They were "Gus" and "Gussie" to each other, but we guess we can forgive them that.

Returning to New York, Augustus gained major critical attention for his work in commemorating heroes of the War Between the States, including two memorials to Robert Gould Shaw, one on the Boston Common and one in his Cornish estate; standing and sitting Abraham Lincolns; and tributes to generals including General John Logan, in Chicago's Grant Park, and William Tecumseh Sherman, in New York's Central Park. The piece that catapulted him to fame was a sculpture of Admiral Farragut, the hero of the Battle of New Orleans. The Farragut statue is on display at the estate.

A young Augustus Saint-Gaudens works at a lathe cutting cameos. *National Park Service/Saint-Gaudens National Historic Site.*

Saint-Gaudens's friend and attorney Charles Beaman was also a patron of the arts. He had ties to northern Vermont and New Hampshire because of his wife, according to Burlingame, and his desire was to see an artists' colony in the North Country.

"Saint-Gaudens was at work on his 'Standing Lincoln' at the time," Burlingame says. "But he had a hard time finding a model in New York. Beaman told him, 'Come to Cornish. It's the land of Lincoln-shaped faces.'"

Beaman bought an old inn turned into a farmhouse. He later built his own property down the road and rented his first property to the Saint-Gaudenses. Augustus, reluctant to leave New York, was unimpressed. "They arrived in mud season, taking the train to Windsor, Vermont, a nine-hour trip, and then a horse and buggy," Burlingame says. "She liked it right away, but he was apprehensive, later writing, 'I thought skeletons were dangling from the windows.'"

But they took the chance, and while summering in the home, Saint-Gaudens and his wife had a taste of the Granite State. Saint-Gaudens also found Langdon Morse, a local man who was his model for Abraham Lincoln in *The Standing Lincoln*, also called *Lincoln, The Man*. Morse, of Windsor, Vermont, was a farmer and had the craggy features Saint-Gaudens was looking for. Lincoln's former tailor was still alive, and Saint-Gaudens engaged him to make a suit for Morse and then had Morse walk around a field "to get that disheveled look," according to Burlingame.

Saint-Gaudens finished the piece within two years, a record for him, Burlingame notes. "He was a perfectionist, and it usually took longer." The peace, quiet and calm of Cornish helped with his work, she says, and he began to look more closely at New Hampshire.

In 1891, the couple purchased the house and used it as their summer retreat. He christened the property Aspet, after his father's birthplace in France.

The Cornish Art Colony formed around Saint-Gaudens, like a snowball. Famous and aspiring artists bought their own summer homes or stayed at Aspet. "When he showed up, they followed," Burlingame says.

The Saint-Gaudenses retained cordial ties with the town, according to Burlingame. They hired locals to farm and groom their hillside acreage, though their maids and cooks came from Boston. Augusta, who managed the money, bought lamp oil and other necessities from North Country vendors, Burlingame says.

Augustus was genial and gregarious, a quality he received from his French father. He was more likely than his wife to interact with the townspeople. His son Homer wrote in a memoir that his father "cared genuinely" for the local people, though their ways were strange to him in the beginning. He would eat at the kitchen table with the servants, a fact that annoyed his gently reared wife. But he enjoyed his servants and his craggy-faced neighbors. "Artists," Burlingame says, "look at people differently."

The town famously protected another resident, the author J.D. Salinger. Residents never told visitors where he lived, even after his death. It was different with Saint-Gaudens, who was already surrounded with people, Burlingame notes.

The stately white brick house still looks out over meadows and the not-too-distant Mount Ascutney in Vermont. The estate has a barn-studio, extensive gardens and sweeping hilltop views. More than one hundred of his pieces, including the Robert Gould Shaw Memorial and a brooding Lincoln, can be seen at the Cornish property, now administered by the National Park Service. The figures are available in a series of "outdoor rooms," defined by shrubbery, and in several pavilions.

Saint-Gaudens was a fierce taskmaster and hardest on himself. Though critically acclaimed pieces of his were scattered around the world, in parks and museums, he was always tweaking to see if he could make them better. Many

Left: The "Standing Lincoln" was completed in Cornish, with a local man as model. *National Park Service/Saint-Gaudens National Historic Site.*

Below: The Saint-Gaudenses purchased this Cornish house as a summer home and named it Aspet. *National Park Service/Saint-Gaudens National Historic Site.*

Saint-Gaudens and his assistants in the Large Studio, 1905. *National Park Service/Saint-Gaudens National Historic Site.*

of those pieces ended up at Aspet, notably his Robert Gould Shaw relief. He was commissioned to make the first installation for the Boston Common, in honor of Shaw's commanding of the Fifty-Fourth Massachusetts Regiment, an all-Black regiment in the Civil War. Though it took the perfectionist fourteen years, Saint-Gaudens did it and collected his commission. But he wasn't satisfied and went back to the chisel. His subsequent version can be seen at the estate, and he preferred it to the first.

The relief is stunning in one way: each Black soldier has a different face. It's a stern reminder to Northerners as to what they fought for.

Diagnosed with cancer in 1900, Saint-Gaudens decided to live out his life in Cornish. "He was," Burlingame says, "done with the city." But it could scarcely be called a retirement or even a retreat. He continued to work and continued to gather other artists around him, including Maxfield Parrish and Isadora Duncan, in what was permanently christened the Cornish Colony. They all had homes nearby, connected by paths, and the visitor could while away an afternoon with a nine-hole golf course, lawn bowling or ice hockey in the winter.

"He knew he was dying, and he chose to live here," Burlingame says.

The family in their first summer in Cornish, 1885. *National Park Service/Saint-Gaudens National Historic Site.*

A double row of birch trees flanks a path at the Saint-Gaudens Historic Site in Cornish. *Sheila Bailey.*

Aspet today. *Sheila Bailey.*

Saint-Gaudens died in 1907. Augusta and their son Homer continued to live on the property. It was deeded to the National Park Service in 1965 and remains New Hampshire's only national park.

His pieces can be found in museums, but the summer home is anything but. The Cornish Colony is alive and vibrant in twenty-first-century garb. The facility hosts workshops for professional artists, summer STEAM camps for teens and a summer concert series.

THE WAY WE WERE

These and other historic homes give a glimpse into the way people lived—in the 603 way. These are not the Newport mansions. As with the Lucknow estate, the owners put in modern conveniences where they could. But they are, first of all, homes.

Chapter 6

MONADNOCK REGION

HARRISVILLE: WEAVING THE FUTURE

The city of Keene anchors the western Monadnock region with a wide main street, interesting shops, cultural resources and, oh yeah, a branch of the state university system. But there's another side to Monadnock West with the smaller towns, strung like beads on a necklace and each with its own specialty and mood. Stoddard was an eighteenth-century hub for glassmaking. Nelson saw the birth of the modern contra dance movement. Swanzey offers an annual production of *The Old Homestead*, written by early resident Denman Thompson. Munsonville has the crystalline Granite Lake. And then there's Harrisville, an early mill village painstakingly restored by its own people.

HARRISVILLE FOR HARRISVILLE

Erin Hammerstedt, former executive director of Historic Harrisville (she has moved to a new position at Shaker Village since this interview), knows exactly what her facility is—and what it is not. "We are not a tourist attraction," she says firmly. "We are not a museum." Hammerstedt has spent her life in historic preservation, and she knows the difference.

"There are no artifacts on shelves or display cases," she says from her office inside the former Mill Number One. "There is nothing for tourists to do inside the buildings." There isn't even shopping, except for the Harrisville General Store and the retail outlet for Harrisville Designs, a fabric company.

The village is by Harrisville for Harrisville.

Hammerstedt works out of one of the old mills. Her office is cool on a hot day, the old stone and old brick dark and sheltering. It's not hard to imagine the machines whirring. Hammerstedt leads the way to a worktable and proceeds to explain her Harrisville and why it's unique.

HISTORY OF HARRISVILLE

Harrisville was first known by the picturesque name of Twitchel's Mills. Abel Twitchel built a combination sawmill and gristmill in 1774, and the village grew up around it. Jason Harris built a blacksmith shop. Jonas Clark built the first textile mill, for fulling and "dressing" cloth. His wife spun linen thread in the same mill. James Horsley bought the Clarks' mill in 1804. The mill had its own wool carding machine, one of only two in the country. In 1822, Bethuel and Cyrus Harris built a brick mill specifically for the manufacture of wool, with Milan Harris installing the machinery. In 1833, Milan Harris and A.S. Hutchinson built a new mill on the site of the old grist and sawmill. It would come to be known as the Upper Mill.[30]

Cyrus Harris constructed Cheshire Mill No. 1 in 1848. The mill was unique in that it was made of granite. Adjacent to the mill is Cheshire Mill No. 2, made of red brick in 1859, and Cheshire Mills 3, 4 and 5, built in the early twentieth century.

The actual town was not incorporated until 1870, with land ceded by Marlborough, Dublin, Hancock, Nelson and Roxbury.

The Manchester and Keene Railroad came to town in 1878, and the town boomed. Its heyday, Hammerstedt says, was in the 1870s through '90s. There were three boardinghouses to shelter the French Canadians, Finns and others who flocked to the ready jobs. One boardinghouse housed fifty-six people, she says. It has since been revamped into three apartments.

Harrisville hosted a number of other businesses servicing the mills and their workers, including four stores, a seamstress, a cobbler and a blacksmith. To help the workers unwind, "there were also a couple of pubs," she notes.

And though the textile mills received the most attention, there were smaller mills in Harrisville. The wooden mills churned out items such as clothespins and mop handles. The mill owners were drawn by the abundance of water power coming from Nubanusit Brook, according to her.

Harrisville paid relatively wall, Hammerstedt notes. She's studied the payroll books. In the late nineteenth century, some workers earned $27.50 a month. "But room and board was $7.00 per month," she reminds you.

Above: The Cheshire Mill No. 1 was the centerpiece for a bustling mill town in Harrisville's heyday. *Historic Harrisville Archives.*

Opposite, top: Another view of the Cheshire Mill No. 1. *Historic Harrisville Archives.*

Opposite, bottom: A worker pauses in the weaving room at the former Cheshire Mill in Harrisville. *Historic Harrisville Archives.*

She's found little evidence of unrest and no records of strikes, "although they came close a couple of times." But when a worker was discontented, all they had to do was walk down the street to another mill or head to the relatively bright lights of Manchester or Lowell.

"It was probably dirty, smelly and noisy," she adds cheerfully.

But the twentieth century brought struggles, and ultimately closing, to the Harrisville mills. Cheshire Mill No. 1 was the last holdout, closing its doors in 1970. Hammerstedt says, "The industry was changing. Double-

The Cheshire Mill building today. *Historic Harrisville Archives.*

knit fabrics were replacing woven fabrics." Cheshire Mill No. 1 hung on. Its owners, the Colony family, subsidized it out of their private funds."

"That's the number one reason why the transition was so successful," Hammerstedt believes. "There was no outside lender beating down the doors. We had time to strategize."

The residents of Harrisville wouldn't let go of their heritage.

"CONCERTED EFFORT"

Hammerstedt explains it like this: "When the mill closed, the community made a concerted effort to preserve the town. The mill company was bankrupt. Fortunately, the owners had time to distribute their assets."

What didn't distribute well were six buildings deemed not marketable. A half dozen residents spanning several generations got together to figure out Harrisville's next move. "The Colony family, who owned the mill, were involved along with the Putnams and several others," she says. They met weekly, sometimes twice weekly.

While the committee had nothing against restored villages such as Sturbridge and Strawbery Banke, they had a different future in mind for their town. "They didn't want to be another charity," Hammerstedt explains. While the group organized as a nonprofit, their business model was different from most. The steering committee wanted to see Harrisville thrive financially, with a diverse mix of businesses and residences.[31]

They came up with a plan to rent the mill space out to businesses and the old boardinghouse units as residential. The complex now includes a childcare center, United States Post Office, the former boardinghouses renewed as apartments and Harrisville Designs, a major tenant. "They have their production facility, their retail shop, they give classes and their corporate headquarters is here," Hammerstedt says. Smaller spaces in the mill buildings are rented by architects, attorneys and other professionals.

"There is," she says, "a high demand for rentals."

The town came relatively early to preservation, with the historic district added to the National Register of Historic Places in 1971 and declared a National Historic Landmark in 1977. The restored Cheshire Mills are

The current Cheshire Mill building, home to small businesses and a textile factory. *Historic Harrisville Archives.*

Catholic Church, Library and Wm. B. McClellan's Store, Harrisville, N. H.

The Harrisville General Store has been a store since 1832 and is now part of Historic Harrisville. *Historic Harrisville Archives.*

The Harrisville General Store runs a full-service bakery and coffee shop, serves breakfast and lunch and Friday-night dinners and serves as a meeting place for the community. *Historic Harrisville Archives.*

protected as part of the Harrisville Historic District and maintained by Historic Harrisville Inc.

Historic Harrisville also owns the general store, a meeting place for the community since 1832. The stone steps are worn from a century of footsteps. Inside, mismatched tables and chairs host locals who lunch. A bustling deli counter offers breakfast and lunch, with dinner added on Fridays. The shelves brim with local maple products, jams and jellies, honey and crafts. There's coffee, tea and a lending library. The deli staff greet customers by name, whenever possible.

NO PLACE LIKE HOME

Some of the cheerful baristas also live in town, according to Hammerstedt. The corporation rents out its apartments at market rate but offers a 20 percent discount to people who work in Harrisville or have retired from work in Harrisville. She explains, "People who live and work in the community are more engaged."

Though she's got a handle on the past, Hammerstedt isn't sure what the future holds. She and the board are engaged in strategic planning. They currently own three buildings that are not in use, and they'd like to see them restored and occupied. The infrastructure—stone walls, bridges—is in need of an update, "though that's difficult to fund."

They'll continue to rent out their properties and keep the community vibrant. "Generating income," she says, "is the best way to preserve the past."

Hammerstedt recalls being involved with a statewide professional association for nonprofits and doing a study. "They asked us, 'If you wanted people to come to your town, how long would you say they could spend?'"

Hammerstedt's response: "We're definitely an hour or less. It's counterintuitive."

She encourages visitors to "come on a beautiful day and walk around." But, she adds, "we do what we do for the people who live here."

MADAME SHERRI'S CASTLE

Many rumors and urban legends have grown up around Chesterfield's "Madame Sherri," who lent the town color and verve in the early twentieth century. One has to do with her birth, according to Nick Apostolides, education director for the Forest Society of New Hampshire and narrator of a short film produced by the "American Ruins" series. "It is said that when she was welcomed into the world, a 'corkscrew of light' beamed over Paris," Apostolides notes.[32]

Lynne Borofsky, a member of the Chesterfield Historical Society, made Madame her personal project about ten to fifteen years ago. As a middle school teacher, Borofsky knows how to do research, and she was aided by a treasure-trove of Madame Sherri artifacts compiled by Wayne Carhart, former president of the Brattleboro, Vermont Historical Society. Madame was too big for one town, or state, and her legend spilled over to Vermont.

In a 2019 video produced by the historical society, Borofsky names a "cast of characters" suitable for one of the Broadway plays Sherri costumed.[33] There's Sherri herself, a flamboyant woman used to making things go her way. There's her husband, Andre Relia, formerly Anthony Macaluso, frequently wanted by the law. And there's Charles LeMaire, a gifted costume designer and protégé of Sherri and Relia, who in turn became her protector, until he couldn't do it anymore. Sherri liked, or at least attracted, younger men: Relia was five years younger than she, LeMaire nineteen years younger.

Andre Relia and Madame Sherri. *Chesterfield Historical Society.*

Antoinette "Madame Sherri" Bramare was born in Paris around 1878. A Frenchwoman can be coy about her birthdate, and the woman who was about to become Madame Sherri had a lot of other things going on. She was a dancer and cabaret singer in her home city, where she met her husband, Macaluso. The bootlegger and organized crimester was on the run from the law and using the name of Andre Relia. He was wanted in New York for bribery, blackmail and other infractions of the law. In Paris, he took on the identity of the son of an Italian diplomat and fell in love, or something, with our young cabaret singer. Sherri took up her own alter ego, saying she was descended from Italian royalty. They cohabited and stayed in Paris until the City of Light lost its luster for them, sometime around 1911.

NEW YORK, NEW YORK!

Bramare and Relia eventually ended up in New York City, a bigger backdrop for their talents. He was apprehended by the city police and spent some time in the Tombs, the city jail, until Sherri somehow managed to get him out. They took to the stage, he as a dancer whose expertise was the brutal "Apache dance," and she as a singer. They lived in unwedded bliss until 1916, when they married in Puerto Rico. Returning to Manhattan, they opened the Andre-Sherri costume shop. An apocryphal story has Sherri designing costumes for the Ziegfeld Girls. Whoever her customers were, she had free rein and a wide imagination, resulting in "one outlandish costume after another," according to Apostolides.

Charles LeMaire, Madame Sherri's protégé and later benefactor. *Chesterfield Historical Society.*

LeMaire was a vaudeville performer and producer who was meant for much more. Broke, he joined the Andre/Sherri firm as an apprentice in 1919 and soon began to show equal if not more talent than his benefactors. He invented a technique for painted-on embroidery, which looked like the real thing, and he designed elaborate costumes for the movies and the Barnum and Bailey Circus. Later in life, he was nominated seventeen times for an Academy Award for costume design and later clothed such luminaries as Marilyn Monroe and

Above, from left: Charles Rathbone, Madame Sherri and Charles LeMaire pose at the Beaux Arts Ball in New York City. *Chesterfield Historical Society.*

Opposite, top: Andre Relia and his wife, Madame Sherri, in Puerto Rico in the 1920s. *Chesterfield Historical Society.*

Opposite, bottom: Madame Sherri's Castle in Chesterfield, New Hampshire, before it burned. *Chesterfield Historical Society.*

Joan Collins. He would move from Sherri's protégé to her protector and eventually provider.

In 1917, Andre was hit in a snowstorm by one of those newfangled motor vehicles. You wouldn't think it would go fast enough, but there you are. His eyesight was damaged, and his health declined until his death in 1924 at the age of twenty-seven. An inconsolable Sherri traveled to Chesterfield, New Hampshire, to visit a friend. She found more than comfort and fell in love with the rural landscape.

In 1929, she purchased 588 acres of land with a farmhouse, the Furlong House, already on it. But like many transplants from the city, she wanted to bring the city with her. In 1931, she began design and construction on what would be called Madame Sherri's Castle across the street from the farmhouse.

She spent summers in the Furlong House, without electricity or running water, using a woodstove when she needed heat. Business in the costume shop was still good, according to Borofsky. "Costuming for shows became really big," she observes, because when people couldn't drink at a show during Prohibition, they demanded more from the production.

Sherri was a hands-on builder, according to Borofsky, and she had no formal plan for the house. "She fired many contractors," Borofsky says. She was building a house from scratch at the age of fifty, and she put sticks down on the ground to show her builders what she wanted.

What she wanted would be unlike anything Chesterfield, or the Granite State, had ever seen. There were stairwells and arches and porches, according to Borofsky. On the main floor was a bar, with living trees poking through the ceiling. The floors were covered in furs, while mirrors lined the bathrooms. A long stone staircase, still in existence, led to Madame Sherri's private quarters. She held court from a cobra-backed throne while she presided over parties. Two upstairs bedrooms were especially elaborate, lending heft to a rumor that prostitutes were on the premises. The public rooms were draped in red velvet, showed off expensive pottery and had a player piano, according to Borofsky. "It was," she says, "like a theatrical stage set."

Dave Anderson, director of education for the Forest Society, notes in the *American Ruins* film that Sherri collected her guests at the train station in Brattleboro, Vermont, in a cream-colored Packard touring car. "It was cream with red wheels," Lynne Borofsky amplifies. "She couldn't drive, so she always had a chauffeur," usually an attractive young woman.

Prohibition was made for women like Madame Sherri to flaunt. She held large house parties with bootleg alcohol. But Prohibition eventually ended, and people went back to drinking in bars.

GREEK TRAGEDY II

The costume shop couldn't support Sherri's lifestyle. Her friend and former protégé Charles LeMaire paid the bills until 1957. Madame Sherri was broke and ill. Her house was vandalized, and after she finally moved out, the castle burned to the ground. She was a bit of a hoarder and lived in the farmhouse across the street, with all her possessions, until she could no longer live alone. She wandered around Vermont, staying with various friends in what would now be called couch-surfing. She ended up in a Brattleboro boardinghouse.

"This," Borofsky says, "is where it gets really sad."

A friend, Walter O'Hara, had been supplementing Sherri's funds. But he couldn't do it anymore, and he billed the City of Brattleboro for her care. He also tried to sue LeMaire. LeMaire bought back the castle, now in foreclosure, for $15,000.

LeMaire sold the property to a Vermont artist, Ann Stokes. Stokes was a preservationist, conservationist and LGBTQ activist. Stokes befriended the elderly eccentric and promised to take care of the property. According to Borofsky, "Ann looked at her and said, 'I will take care of your land.'" Stokes

A tumbled chimney hints at former glory in the remains of Madame Sherri's Castle, Chesterfield. *Courtesy C. Symmes/Society for the Protection of New Hampshire Forests.*

Above: The famed "Staircase to Nowhere" at Madame Sherri's Forest in Chesterfield. *Courtesy Anna Berry/Society for the Protection of New Hampshire Forests.*

Right: Madame Sherri, cabaret performer and costume designer, poses for the camera. *Chesterfield Historical Society.*

visited Madame Sherri until the latter's death at the age of eighty-seven, in October 1965, and gave lavish parties in her memory. Stokes owned the land for several years before deeding it to the Forest Society in 1991 and renaming it Madame Sherri Forest.

The Forest Society now manages the property, including several hiking trails. One is named the Ann Stokes Loop. The only vestige of the castle is the stone staircase that survived the house fire in 1962. But the vibe is still there, and one feels, "If only this staircase could talk."

"Her legacy," Dave Anderson says in the *American Ruins* film, "is bigger than life itself."

Chapter 7

SOMEBODY HAD TO BE HIM

THE LIFE, TIMES AND HOMES
OF FRANKLIN PIERCE

New Hampshire residents often "take the fifth" when it comes to the fourteenth. Franklin Pierce, the country's fourteenth president and the only one from the Granite State, was soft on slave states and big on states' rights. He is a tragic figure, when we think of him at all. Some have glibly called him the "worst president ever." But just as no one suggests tearing down Manchester's René Gagnon monument, few people have suggested pulling Pierce's statue from the State House Plaza. While tributes topple all across the nation, no one in the Granite State has seriously suggested removing Pierce.

Pierce is remembered with two restored houses in his home state. His father, Benjamin, moved to New Hampshire from Massachusetts in 1784 and built a sprawling farmhouse in Hillsboro. Franklin was born in 1804.[34]

Benjamin Pierce was a farmer, local militia leader and two-time New Hampshire governor. He trained militia for the Revolution in the second-story ballroom. The home also served as a tavern and place to discuss the fomenting rebellion.

Franklin Pierce attended Bowdoin College and studied law. He returned to Hillsboro in 1827 and established his law practice across the road from the homestead. He was elected to the New Hampshire legislature at the age of twenty-four. The young attorney developed a taste for politics, and by the 1830s, he was in Washington, first as a representative and then as a senator. He married Jane Means Appleton of Amherst in 1834 and lived for a while in Hillsborough. The union produced three sons, none of whom lived to adulthood. They moved to Concord in 1838.[35]

If only he'd stayed in Concord.

This gracious Colonial home provided shelter and nurturing for Benjamin Pierce's large brood, including a future president. *Sheila Bailey.*

The second-floor ballroom at Benjamin Pierce's Hillsboro home was a site for parties, political meetings and more. *New Hampshire Parks and Recreation: Bureau of Historic Sites.*

"BLEEDING KANSAS"

Pierce served in the Mexican War, came home and continued his involvement in politics. He took positions *against* the abolition of slavery and supported the Compromise of 1850, which sought to mollify both sides of the slavery issue in the growing country. The Compromise of 1850 negated the 1820 Missouri Compromise, which had admitted Missouri and Maine to the Union as a slave state and a free state, respectively, and prohibited slavery in the western territories acquired in the Louisiana Purchase north of latitude 36°30'. The new Compromise of 1850 entailed admitting California to the Union as a free state; leaving New Mexico and Utah to decide for themselves; allowing any territory gained after the Mexican-American War to make up its own mind; enacting Fugitive Slave Laws; and abolishing slavery in the District of Columbia. Nobody liked the compromise.

After forty-eight ballots, Pierce was nominated as a "dark horse" candidate by the Democrats in the 1852 presidential election. He won the election but lost his last living child, an eleven-year-old boy, in a train wreck sometime between the election and assuming office. Pierce came to Washington in a cloud of grief and loss. Jane came with a lot less.

Northerners already disliked Pierce for his perceived support of slavery. But the Kansas-Nebraska Act raised passions to a new pitch. Nobody, absolutely nobody, liked the Kansas-Nebraska Act of 1854. In the view of proslavery southerners, the Compromise of 1850 had already repealed the Missouri Compromise by admitting California as a free state, including territory south of the compromise line. The Kansas-Nebraska Act created two new territories, the northern part being Nebraska and the southern territory Kansas, and allowed for popular sovereignty on the topic of slavery. The expectation was that Kansas would allow slavery and Nebraska would not, but it wasn't that simple. Both pro- and anti-slavery activists swarmed into the region. The Kansas border, and parts of western Missouri, became a battleground over the legality of slavery in Kansas. Kansas bled for five years, from 1854 to 1859.

The Democrats did not nominate Pierce for a second term, and he returned to the Granite State bitter and broken. The deaths of his wife and his lifelong friend Nathaniel Hawthorne further depressed him. He died in Concord in 1869, at the age of sixty-four, and is buried in the city's Old North Cemetery.

And Concord spent the next century wondering what to do about him.

AT HOME WITH THE PRESIDENT: THE BIRTHPLACE

The Hillsborough home remained in the hands of various Pierces until 1925, when the State of New Hampshire acquired it. The New Hampshire Federation of Women's Clubs took on the restoration as a project and worked on it from 1945 to 1950. Additional work was done by the state. The site is currently managed by the New Hampshire Division of State Parks. It is a National Historic Landmark and was logged in the Historic American Buildings Survey (HABS).

On a warm summer day, Sara Dobrowolski, manager of the site, leads a group through the gift shop and into the mudroom. The first thing she points out is an iron contraption she calls a "boot jack." "The Pierces hired more help than anyone else in Hillsboro," she says, adding, "But they were egalitarian. Nobody pulled off your boots for you." She shows off a maple sugar mold, shoe molds, baskets and crocks and a small wood planer. "This is for creating 'spills' so you can light a fire," she explains.

The front entrance hall at the Pierce homestead in Hillsboro. *New Hampshire Parks and Recreation: Bureau of Historic Sites.*

As his family grew, Benjamin Pierce added on to the original home. He bought an abandoned farmhouse, had it pulled to the property on a sledge and installed it as a kitchen. He built a second story, where his daughters and the hired girls slept. Being a hired girl was a good gig, Dobrowolski points out: "You got three meals a day, clothes and a roof over your head." The domestic training in a house like Ben's was invaluable, she adds. With few opportunities for girls, if they learned to manage a mansion, they could marry a man who owned a mansion.

The Pierce place was one of the rowdier ones in early Hillsboro, with a tavern in one of the front parlors and frequent comers-and-goers. After the addition in 1812, the old kitchen became the formal dining room. The table could be extended with leaves upon leaves upon leaves and frequently was, according to Dobrowolski: "Benjamin was a self-made man, and he wanted everyone in his house to dine together as equals." This included family, hired girls, hired men and the lone free Black man in Hillsboro. The room has a generous fireplace, a stenciled floorcloth and the original sideboard, dining table, chairs and punch bowl, according to Dobrowolski.

The original hip-roofed home was built in 1804. There are two entrances, one on the west, street-facing side and one on the south. Both are topped

The Pierce Homestead dining room. *New Hampshire Parks and Recreation: Bureau of Historic Sites.*

by five-light transom windows and flanked by pilasters that support an entablature, or horizontal continuous lintel, and triangular pediment. The two-story wing was added to the rear of the house. Attached to this wing are a small wellhouse and a single-story shed connecting the house to a gable-roofed barn.

The original house has a central hall and stairway flanked by four rooms, a parlor to the left and a dining room to the right. The kitchen stands behind the dining room and a master bedroom behind the parlor. The second floor has a ballroom running the length of the front and two bedrooms, each with a dressing room, at the rear. The added wing has a laundry and kitchen area, first floor and servants' rooms on the second. Sons and daughters of the household often bunked in with the servants because "everybody worked in this house," Dobrowolski says.

The elder Pierce was an important man in Hillsboro and the New Hampshire colony and a "huge" influence on his son's life, according to Dobrowolski. His origins were humble. Born in 1757 in Chelmsford, Massachusetts, Ben left home when his new stepmother didn't want him. He stayed briefly with an uncle who also didn't want him. When Ben was seventeen, he heard about the Shot Heard 'Round the World, grabbed his uncle's bird-hunting rifle and was off to the Revolutionary War. He ended the war as a lieutenant, commissioned by one George Washington.

Ben Pierce worked briefly as a land surveyor and finally bought a log cabin and five hundred acres in Hillsboro. He stayed in Chelmsford, coming up summers to clear the land. When he was ready to take a bride, he married Elizabeth Andrews, who gave him one daughter before she died. His second wife, Anna Kendrick, gave him eight more children, including Franklin, the seventh of nine.

Ben was a banker, mortgage broker, landowner, tavern keeper and two-time governor of New Hampshire. He owned land in Goshen that was rich in graphite, a mineral he was able to sell to the Dixon Pencil Company. He was a farmer and, oh yeah, a war hero. "How did a scrawny farm kid from New Hampshire get to be president?" Dobrowolski asks. "Ben was a tough act to follow."

But Ben passed on to Franklin the principles that were to be the younger Pierce's salvation and downfall: a passionate belief in keeping the Union together at all costs. This was the Union Ben had fought to establish, and it was the Union Franklin strove to preserve. "He was a strict Constitutionalist who wanted to avoid the breakup of the Union," Dobrowolski says. "He was personally opposed to slavery, but he wanted to gradually eliminate it."

AT HOME WITH THE PRESIDENT: THE CONCORD HOUSE

The Pierce Manse stands less than a block from Concord's Main Street, but it could have been deep in the country. The sound of vehicles from downtown doesn't reach back here. Waterfowl swoop low over a nearby pond, and a breeze ruffles the ancient trees. With the exception of power lines and parked cars, the Pierce Manse looks much as it did in the nineteenth century.

Jane Pierce never liked Hillsborough, and she persuaded her husband to move the family to Concord. They lived in a house on Montgomery Street from 1842 to 1848. In Concord, Pierce practiced law, served as district attorney and chaired the local Democratic Party. He also served as United States district attorney for New Hampshire, in recognition of his efforts to elect President James K. Polk. Polk later offered Pierce the United States attorney general position, which Pierce declined due to Jane's poor health. Jane didn't like Washington either, but after those forty-eight ballots in 1852, she had no choice. They went, he worked, it didn't work and they came home.

Kat Braden, a volunteer guide at the Manse in Concord, isn't having any of that "worst president" nonsense. As she leads a manse tour, she points to some of Pierce's accomplishments, rattling them off with ease: "He improved relations with Britain and Canada. He fostered the western expansion, including along the U.S.-Mexico border and the Transcontinental Railroad. He reduced the nation's debt, fostered trade with Japan and reformed the civil service and its hiring policies."

After a pause for breath, Braden adds, "But that was all overshadowed by the Kansas-Nebraska Act."

Pierce had only one term in Washington. He left immediately on an extended tour of Europe, where Jane blossomed, briefly, and the family had a chance to heal. He returned in 1858, just in time for the War Between the States. Though technically retired, Pierce remained a vocal critic of the government in terms of its alleged violating the Constitution and the Bill of Rights. Loyal to his friends, he helped effect Jefferson Davis's release from prison after the war. After his old friend Nathaniel Hawthorne died, Pierce put Hawthorne's son through college. "He had a beautiful, loving soul," Braden muses.

Jane Pierce died in 1863. Franklin died in Concord in 1869, in a house on South Main Street that burned in 1981.

THE PIERCE BRIGADE

Just beyond mid-century, the concept of urban renewal stuck its claws into several 603 towns.[36] In 1966, Concord's renewal program threatened Pierce's South End home, where he had lived pre-presidency. Concord didn't always get historic preservation right, especially in the early years.[37] But a grassroots organization, the Pierce Brigade, formed and raised funds to keep the president's home. City officials deemed the house "not worth saving," according to a pamphlet detailing the history of the Brigade. But the Brigade-ers were more than a match for city hall.[38]

Polly B. Johnson, one of the original Brigade members, wrote in a pamphlet: "It took considerable perseverance by a small band of interested and dedicated citizens to accomplish this, since there were those in public positions who thought a simple granite marker or a bronze plaque on the site would carry as much significance to honor Franklin Pierce as a restored home."[39]

Schoolchildren win a contest as part of the Pierce Brigade's promotional efforts. The reason for the contest is lost in the mists of time, but the kids did their part. *Alfred Perron.*

Opposite, top: Part of the gala 1971 parade moving the Pierce home from the South End to the North. *Alfred Perron.*

Opposite, bottom: A horse-drawn carriage helps create the spirit as the Pierce Brigade parades from the Pierce Manse's former home on Montgomery Street to its new dig at Horseshoe Pond on July 14, 1971. *Alfred Perron.*

Above: The Pierce Manse, the only home President Franklin Pierce owned when he lived in Concord, is now preserved and open to the public thanks to a group known as the Pierce Brigade. *Sheila Bailey.*

The Brigade received a boost in January 1969, when the Pierce Manse made the National Register of Historic Places, due to an application by the New Hampshire Commission on Resources and Economic Development. It was the first New Hampshire property to be entered in the register.

The Brigade attacked fundraising with particular vigor, conducting rummage, bake, book and candy sales. Offered the use of a downtown storefront, they put up a "Pierce for President" sign and solicited Concord residents for donations. There were missteps and setbacks, including $38,000 of federal money earmarked for Concord going to the Laconia Belknap Mill project instead of the Manse.

But the Brigade hung in there, gathering members and recognition for their cause. The building was loaded on to a flatbed truck and moved from

Montgomery Street to Penacook Street, now Horseshoe Pond Lane, in 1971. Women dressed in period costumes for an impromptu parade. Johnson went as Jane Pierce, and Ernest Freeman rode on horseback as Brigadier General Franklin Pierce. After extensive restoration of the interior, the house opened to the public in 1974.

The house is classically proportioned and more urban and formal than the Hillsborough property. Several pieces of Pierce family furniture survive, including the desk from his Concord law office and a sofa that was part of Jane's dowry. A crystal chandelier hangs over a table set with a replica of the Pierces' White House china. On the mantelpiece, two candle holders made of crystal prisms catch the late afternoon sunshine. With delight, Braden opens a cupboard and brings out a carefully framed scrap of the room's original wallpaper. She shows off Franklin's top hat and walking stick, a table from the White House years, shelves of books and other mementoes.

A sign in one of the rooms says it all, according to Braden: "He was faithful to the Constitution and true to the Union."

HISTORY HAS ALREADY JUDGED HIM

Pierce's two homes and his statue continue to stand. While he has few actual fans outside of the Brigade, and few people who will admit to supporting his views, we won't tear down his stuff. We don't do that kind of thing in New Hampshire.

There's a parallel with René Gagnon, the Manchester marine who let the public think he was one of the flag-raisers at Iwo Jima. He wasn't, as an update from the Marines told us in 2019. While René was gone by then, the city and state had to figure out what to do with the sin of omission. In the end, we went with what we had. Disclaimers went up in any venue where he could be disclaimed. Historical society exhibits got tweaked. But the installation in Manchester's Victory Park stayed. He was still a hero—just not the hero we thought he was. We thought it through.[40]

And that may be the key to Franklin Pierce. He meant well. If he were alive, nobody would ever hire him to speak at a Diversity Dinner. If he wrote an op-ed for the *New Hampshire Union Leader* or the *Concord Monitor*, it would be savaged. But we've let him go, with a shrug and a knowledge that if New Hampshire sends another man or woman to the White House, we'll think it through.

It is what we do.

Chapter 8

IN PLAIN SIGHT

THE HOMES OF PORTSMOUTH

New Hampshire cherishes its history as much as any place in the country. We have to; there's so much of it. After a few hiccups in the nineteenth and early twentieth centuries and some stunning losses ("urban renewal"), Granite Staters got wise to the treasures in our midst. Historic preservation lurched to a beginning. One early example was in Exeter, when townspeople rallied in 1970 to save the historic Sleeper House from being razed and replaced with a bank. Exeter "got it" from that point forward. Nearly every home and business in the historic Water Street area bears a brass plate letting you know who lived there and when.

Portsmouth takes it a step further. Its historic homes sport brass plates touting their provenance—but more than a dozen, including the renowned Strawbery Banke, are open to the public and provide a window into another life.

WARNER HOUSE

Stephanie Hewson, site manager for the Warner House, enjoys conducting tours of the Grande Dame of Daniel Street. One of her favorite rooms is the upstairs ballroom, which shows original owner Archibald MacPheadris's money *and* ambition.

One upstairs bedroom received a wall treatment known as "smalt." This involved crushed cobalt blue glass strewn onto paint while it was still tacky.

The Warner House is the Grande Dame of Daniel Street. *Sheila Bailey.*

In 2004, the smalt treatment was re-created in the restored Jonathan Warner bedchamber. The room was also used as an office—and a ballroom. Hewson gestures for visitors to look closely at the walls. "It sparkles," she says, adding, "Can you imagine that under a chandelier and by candlelight? It shimmers."

Smalt was expensive, and most Portsmouth gentry confined its use to the woodwork. "But MacPheadris had it everywhere," she says with a smile.

Welcome to the world of the wealthy Portsmouth businessman.

The Warner House was built in 1716 for MacPheadris, a Scots-Irish sea captain who first worked out of Boston before moving north. Portsmouth was the home of his future bride, Sarah Wentworth, daughter of Lieutenant Governor John Wentworth. It was the earliest urban brick home built in northern New England.[41]

John Drew (1675–1738) served as MacPheadris's builder. Drew learned the building trade in London in the early 1700s. He arrived in Boston after the Great Boston Fire of 1711. The Warner House Association still has the bill for his services, dated 1716 and in meticulous detail, including the number of stairs leading up to the cupola.

A bedroom in the Warner House. *Sheila Bailey.*

The two-and-a-half-foot-thick walls are made of local brick, with every 1,000th brick stamped "NH." The house originally had a steeply pitched roof. It worked well in the rainy climate of the Mother Country. But in New England, the pitch resulted in ice buildup and then leakage when it melted. The roof was replaced with a gambrel style, though the original pitched roof can still be seen in the attic.

In addition to being a ship's owner and captain, MacPheadris was a successful land speculator, investor in the first ironworks in New Hampshire and member of the King's Council. He was something of a character, once bringing a four-month-old female lion home from Cadiz, Spain. It was the first known lion in the Colonies.

He and Sarah had three children, Sarah, Mary and Gilbert. Sarah's namesake died in infancy.

He also owned land across Daniel Street, which he filled with gardens and outbuildings, according to Hewson. "He wanted," she says, "to show off what he'd accomplished."

And show off he did, especially in the front staircase.

WHAT'S ON *YOUR* WALLS?

The murals in the entrance hall are considered the earliest extant British-American wall paintings in America. MacPheadris commissioned the murals shortly after he moved in. The painting of the murals has been attributed by some scholars to Portsmouth-born Nehemiah Partridge, a New York–based artist whose father was lieutenant governor of New Hampshire.

"The reasoning behind them," Hewson says cheerfully, "is a mystery."

MacPheadris died in 1729, and subsequent occupants covered the side murals with wallpaper. The two Mohawk sachems on the landing were never covered. In 1853, Sherburne grandchildren were playing on the stairs, and one pulled off a length of wallpaper. Under several layers of wallpaper, the child discovered the forgotten murals.

Perhaps because MacPheadris was a sea captain, birds are a frequent motif in the murals. Other themes are biblical, such as the story of Abraham and Isaac. The Mohawk sachems represent two of the four Native Americans presented in Queen Anne's court in 1710.

Another mystery is the identity of a male figure on horseback, wearing a gold crown and with a *P* emblazoned on his document bag. Historians

Two Mohawk sachems flank the landing window at the Warner House in Portsmouth. *Sheila Bailey.*

This whimsical scene of a woman spinning and a mischievous canine is one of the murals in the Warner House. *Sheila Bailey.*

theorize that the image might portray Prince William, the Duke of Gloucester, second in line to the British throne, and Hewson tends to agree.

Other scenes and vignettes invite puzzlement, including a picture of a woman spinning and a runaway dog. She's not a royal personage or a biblical or classical figure, so Hewson speculates she might be something domestic that happened around the house.

SIX GENERATIONS

Archibald MacPheadris died in 1729, and his widow and two children remained in the home until Sarah remarried. Sarah remarried well, to George Jaffrey II, chief justice of the New Hampshire Supreme Court. She moved down the street to the Jaffrey House (no longer in existence). She rented her former house out until 1741, when her brother Royal Governor Benning Wentworth moved in. Wentworth used the house as his Governor's Mansion and repeatedly petitioned the Provincial Assembly to purchase it, but they couldn't or wouldn't meet Sarah's price, and he eventually permanently retired to his home at Little Harbor.

Archibald's daughter Mary lived in the home through her first marriage to John Osborne Jr., who left her under unexplained circumstances. A wealthy heiress, she remarried to Jonathan Warner, a successful Portsmouth merchant, and the "Warner" came into the Warner House. After Mary's death, he married another wealthy heiress, Elizabeth Pitts, in 1781. Elizabeth died in 1810, leaving him *her* vast estate. The Sherburne family came into the picture in 1814, after Jonathan Warner's death, when he left his property to his niece Elizabeth Warner Sherburne and her son, John Nathaniel Sherburne. Six generations of MacPheadrises, Warners and Sherburnes eventually enjoyed the property, well into the twentieth century.

The house underwent alterations, modifications and even modernization, which had to be beat back when it opened as a museum. In the early 1930s, the property went up for sale. An oil company had the house in its sights to raze the property and raise up a gas station. Portsmouth wasn't having any. An organization developed, the Warner House Association, and purchased the property in 1932. The house opened as a museum that same summer.

The last of the family members took or sold just about everything in the house, but that didn't faze the new association. "We managed to get 70 percent of it back," Hewson says.

The house includes elegant woodwork, blue-and-white or rust-and-white tiles around the fireplaces and four-poster beds draped in pricey textiles. The restored master bedroom sports green damask hangings, a tiled fireplace and a table and chairs, because colonials often entertained in their bedrooms. A powdered wig waits on a special stand.

In the front parlor, a seven-foot-high secretary holds hundreds of books, most belonging to Polly, Jonathan Warner's daughter by his first marriage. "It's unusual," Hewson muses, "for a girl to have that many books." Woodworker Robert Harrold created the secretary for that house and that spot. "It has never been moved," Hewson says. "When we want to change things, we work around it."

Even the tiniest detail shows the owners' ambitions. In the front parlor, there's a small stand holding an urn for tea-making. "It's showing off," Hewson notes, "that they could afford a piece of furniture that only does one thing."

THE MOFFATT-LADD HOUSE

The Moffatt-Ladd House on Market Street has not only its own provenance but also the provenance of a tree in its yard. Guide Lauren Gianino points out that the massive horse chestnut was planted in 1776, when resident William Whipple returned from signing the Declaration of Independence. Whipple and his enslaved companion, a man named Prince, hauled the sapling back from Philadelphia and planted it in the front yard.

These were family homes, and the families lived in them as long as they could. The Moffatt-Ladd House was built between 1760 and 1763 for Samuel and Catherine Moffatt. Samuel was the only son of John Moffatt, one of the wealthiest men in the colony before the Revolution. The younger Moffatts moved in in February 1764, and that was the beginning of almost 150 years of residence by Moffatts and Ladds.[42]

John Moffatt, who built the house for his son, was a successful merchant and wanted to show his wealth through the house. Coming to America as a ship's captain, he became one of the richest men in the New Hampshire colony. He dealt in fabric, china, glass, firearms and enslaved people,

The Moffatt-Ladd House on Market Street in Portsmouth. *Sheila Bailey.*

according to Gianino. He also dealt in timber and made a fortune off a Europe "starved" for timber.

Michael Whidden III was the lead builder, along with eleven joiners and several of Moffatt's enslaved people. Whidden would also construct the counting house, barn and fences for the estate.

The three-story home was the first of that height in Portsmouth, and raising it brought special challenges, as it was destined for a slope. The red pine was milled from Moffatt's own land up north, notched at the site and ferried down the river by gundalow. The house included an attic and a basement containing a wine cellar, a buttery, a summer kitchen and a private well.

The house was adorned with carving: medallions, rosettes, stair carvings and capitals, among others. Ebenezer Dearing submitted a bill for the craft work.

Visitors entered through the great hall, to a room stretching over one-quarter of the first floor and dominated by a sweeping staircase with carved soffits. The staircase features the trio of carved balusters known as the "Portsmouth style," also seen in the Warner House.

An elegant dining area at the Moffatt-Ladd House. *Sheila Bailey.*

The kitchen features the original dresser, built in 1763 to hold china. "Think of all the hands who have touched this piece," Gianino muses. "Enslaved people, Irish servants."

The Yellow Room, or "best chamber," survives unaltered as an example of the house's elegance. The wallpaper, with its hunting scenes, was in the latest fashion. The room boasted yellow damask bed hangings, window hangings, window seat cushions and upholstered furniture. It was meant to be seen, and house historians speculate that it was the room where female guests came to rest from the partying or primp for more.

"Your bed hangings," Gianino says, "were the second-most expensive things you owned. The first was your silver."

But Samuel, alas, was not a good businessman. An ill-fated slavery venture with his brother-in-law Peter Livius threw this into relief. Most of the enslaved persons on the *Triton* died during the passage from Africa to the West Indies. Livius sued Samuel for his share of the venture, and Samuel fled to the Dutch-held island of St. Eustatius. Sarah Catherine joined him there in 1769. She left two of her children behind with her sister-in-law Katharine Moffatt, who moved into the mansion and held it in a death grip.

Katharine married William Whipple, a Portsmouth businessman, ship's captain and signer of the Declaration of Independence. Here Portsmouth's White history intersects with its Black history, at least on paper: William Whipple's enslaved manservant was a Black man named Prince.

Prince Whipple accompanied William to Philadelphia and back and most likely heard much of the rhetoric behind the Declaration. In 1779, he and eighteen other men, including John Moffatt's slave Windsor Moffatt, petitioned the legislature for their freedom. It was determined that one of the petitioners not only was literate but also used language similar to that in Revolutionary documents. Historians point to Prince Whipple.

But Prince wasn't done yet. In 1781, he married a free Black woman, Dinah Chase, and in 1784, William Whipple signed his freedom papers. Katharine Whipple deeded a plot of land to Prince Whipple and Cuffee Whipple, another free Black man, and they moved onto it with their wives, Dinah and Rebecca. The men continued to work, for wages this time, and Dinah and Rebecca Whipple started the African Ladies Charitable School.

MEANWHILE, BACK AT THE MANSION...

Sarah Catherine Moffatt and Katharine Whipple feuded, bitterly and energetically, over the property. The house passed into the hands of Nathaniel Haven in 1818 and, one year later, to his daughter Maria Tufton Haven Ladd. The house was to remain in Ladd hands until 1911.

The Ladds made changes to the house, including a warehouse and other outbuildings. They converted the front parlor to a dining room. They repapered the walls of the great hall and staircase with wallpaper in the *Vues d'Italie* pattern.

The other parlor was comfortably furnished in the Victorian fashion. A marble-topped pier table and glass shared the space with a hair sofa and two antique armchairs, in the Chinese export style, possibly purchased from the Wentworth estate by Nathaniel Haven in 1794.

Alexander Hamilton or "A.H." Ladd assumed ownership of the house in 1861. He made many modern improvements, including an extensive drainage system, updated stoves and a combination refrigerator/ dumbwaiter. He added a working toilet. He also kept the formal gardens in

The gardens at the Moffatt-Ladd House. *Sheila Bailey.*

top shape, with a particular interest in tulips. Some of the plants in Ladd's garden date back as far as 1765.

He, too, was a colorful character, according to Gianino. He made his money as a cotton broker in Galveston, Texas. He once killed a whale in Portsmouth Harbor, and he was fond of big-game hunting, decorating the house with his animal heads.

When A.H. Ladd died in 1900, his family inherited the home and lived there on and off for eleven years. In 1911, the heirs offered the home to the National Society of Colonial Dames of America, with the provision that it be preserved as a museum and maintained as the group's headquarters for New Hampshire. The Dames have done that, seeking out original furniture or Portsmouth pieces from the period. They honor the memory of both the wealthy White families who owned it and the enslaved people who toiled there. Gianino moves a curtain to show off a barely there etching in a pane of ancient glass: the poem "Roses are red, violets are blue."

"Polly Tufton Moffatt, Samuel's daughter, did that," she says. "Her father was a fugitive, and she was raised here by her aunt and uncle."

WENTWORTH-GARDNER

Mary Sullivan, a tour guide at the Wentworth-Gardner House, urges visitors to pause for a minute on the stone steps of the mansion before going inside. It takes just a little imagination to "see" exactly how it was in the eighteenth century: carriages going by instead of cars, peddlers instead of the iconic Geno's Coffee Shop and the mighty Piscataqua River bringing merchant ships up to the dock instead of motorboats and kayaks.

"We are here," she says, "because of the Piscataqua. The Abenakis worked the river thousands of years before. The British, Spanish, French and Portuguese fished in these waters."

But by 1760, Portsmouth was a vibrant commercial community, and the Wentworth family owned the river frontage.

The Wentworth-Gardner House, built in 1760, is one of the finest examples of Georgian architecture not only in the city but also in the country, according to its website. It was a wedding gift from Mark Hunkins Wentworth and his wife, Elizabeth Ridge Wentworth, to their son Thomas and his wife, Anne. The Wentworth family was a powerful force in the early years of the colony. Colonial Governor Benning Wentworth was an uncle, and Thomas's brother John Wentworth served as the last royal governor.[43]

The Wentworth-Gardner House has a storied history on Portsmouth's waterfront. *Sheila Bailey.*

The Georgian style was based on Greek and Roman style, with its symmetry and composition, Sullivan says, squinting in the sunlight as she points up to the pineapple decoration above the front door. The doors and windows are in the Palladian style, after the Roman architect Palladio, who studied classical architecture before producing his own pattern book.

But more than that, the Georgian style harkens back to Merrie Olde England, and that is what prominent Portsmouth families, at least the Loyalists, wanted, according to Sullivan. "They wanted," she says, "to re-create England."

Sullivan leads the way into the generous entrance hall. She points out the crown moldings and other woodwork and their variety—dentil molding, egg-and-dart carvings. The hall's molding is the work of one Eben Deering, a shipbuilder, she points out.

The elaborate newel post is by a different artist, Richard Miles, she says. And the stair balusters are what would be known as the Portsmouth style, with three different patterns alternating their way up the grand staircase. There's more molding, a lot of it, around the fireplaces in the two front parlors. The fireplaces don't have mantels, so there is room for more carving. Though she sees it every day they're open, Sullivan muses, "It is incredible woodwork."

The North Parlor has blue-and-white tile around its hearth. The casual viewer might think it Delft, Sullivan notes. But it isn't. "This is Bristol tile, made in Bristol, England," she says. It was used by the finest families and hearkened back to Merrie Olde.

Eben Deering also did the woodwork on the fireplace in the other front parlor, an intricate arrangement of flowers known as the "rose frieze."

Everything, she says, speaks to a wealthy colonial family bent on showing their wealth. How rich were they? This branch of Wentworths owned ships, warehouses, other businesses and a swath of land in Wolfeboro bordering Lake Winnipesaukee.

Thomas and Elizabeth had five children and raised them in the mansion. After her death in 1768, he and his second wife, Anne, decamped for England.

An Ichabod Nichols bought the house in 1779. He was a privateer, or "legalized pirate," according to Sullivan. He had twelve children, nine of whom were born in the Mechanic Street house.

The elegant staircase at the Wentworth-Gardner House features woodwork including a style of baluster unique to colonial Portsmouth. *Sheila Bailey.*

The elaborate tiling on this Wentworth-Gardner fireplace looks like Delft but was made in England. *Sheila Bailey.*

The dentil molding, the high ceilings and the tiled fireplaces still stand and speak of wealth. But most of all, Sullivan muses, "these were *homes*."

Ichabod's son George later became a sea captain and still later wrote an autobiography. Sullivan has been reading it online and says the book gives the reader a full picture of what went on in the Mechanic Street mansion, at least from a small boy's perspective. George writes of "coasting," or sledding, down the front yard and over the street into the not-yet-frozen Piscataqua. "He says at least ten times he almost drowned," she reports with a smile.

George also recounts the story of when he surprised his mother baking gingerbread. "She told him, 'This is not fit for a dog,'" Sullivan recounts. Young George wasn't fooled, and he kept sneaking chunks and slices of the spicy treat over the next week. His mother was appalled when she hosted several women for tea and the treat she'd baked and saved was gone.

George, in short, was a character.

The "Gardner" part of the name came in 1793, when Major William Gardner bought the house. He lived there with his second wife, Elizabeth. Major Gardner occupied the house for forty years, until his death at eighty-three. His third wife, Sarah Purcell Gardner, lived there until 1854.

The house was to pass through several more sets of hands, including the Peirces of Peirce Island fame and one Captain Drowne. By 1900, it was fairly run-down and had also suffered several Victorian "improvements," according to Sullivan.

Here's where the Wentworth-Gardner House dovetails with one of the major twentieth-century restoration movements. Enter Wallace Nutting.

Nutting was a photographer, antique collector, historian and restoration expert. His passion was restoring Colonial homes to their Colonial glory, and he couldn't resist the Wentworth-Gardner. He purchased it in 1915. Nutting was the father of the Colonial Revival movement and the savior of the Wentworth Gardner.

Nutting began peeling away Victorian (and worse) wallpaper. He sourced furnishings as close to the originals as possible. He walled in two Victorian-era doors. He found a Colonial-era house that was being torn down and snagged the original wallpaper for the Wentworth-Gardner dining room. And he used the house for his own photo staging of Colonial scenes. Several of these are on display in the house. He even put in an early twentieth-century sink and toilet to use while he worked. This and a downstairs modern bathroom are anachronistic, Sullivan cheerfully admits. "The necessary," she says, was actually on the back corner of the lot.

Nutting opened the house briefly as a museum while he continued to work on it. But even Wallace Nutting couldn't hang on to things forever.

With the advent of World War I, people weren't traveling, and they didn't have their minds on historic houses. In 1918, Nutting put the house on the market. It was purchased by no less than the Metropolitan Museum of Art in New York City. The Met prized the house as a near-perfect example of Georgian architecture and made plans to have it moved to the city. But the stock market crash of 1929 put an end to that deal. Even the Met had its limits.

The Society for the Preservation of New England Antiquities (then SPNEA, now Historic New England) purchased the house, furnished it and briefly operated it as a house museum. The house was back in New England hands. But even New England control couldn't beat local control.

Portsmouth was an early endorser of historic preservation, saving the Warner House from a gas station and recognizing the value of its historic houses while other towns were paving Paradise and putting in parking lots. The Colonial Dames saved the Moffatt-Ladd House from the wrecking ball as early as 1911. And a group of determined residents purchased the

Wentworth-Gardner House in 1940. They formed the Wentworth-Gardner Historic House Association, which today owns and operates the property.

Sullivan shows off a cozy kitchen with a large dresser displaying china and a huge fireplace. A wooden bread trough waits in front of the fireplace. The servants' stairs are behind a door, and she points out the worn place in the middle of each step. "You can see the place where their toes hit," Sullivan says, "hundreds and hundreds of steps over the years."

A huge Palladian window anchors the second floor, topped with a carving that might possibly be Queen Charlotte. Another window has a small table, two chairs and a tea set and overlooks the river. "Imagine sitting here," Sullivan says, "and watching the tall ships go by."

The bedrooms boast four-poster beds and fireplaces. In the master bedroom, the bed is taller, and the fireplace has even more carving—flowers, curlicues, Greek key designs. It also has extra columns to the side. "Just look at the work," Sullivan marvels.

But Sullivan never loses sight of whose house she's showing. "I was a history major in college, and I've always felt a connection to people," she says as she leads the way down the wide central staircase. "I want to know more and more about them." She's currently fascinated with young George and his exploits, noting, "He was always protecting his older brother" (a milder-mannered young person who became a minister). "One time when the teacher pulled his brother's ear, George threw a Bible at him."

And she'll happily insert "her" family members into the appropriate settings. Recalling the kitchen, she says, "That's the kitchen where George's mother made the gingerbread!"

CODA

Downtown Portsmouth replicates the feeling I have at Lexington and Concord, especially Lexington. In Lexington, residents toss frisbees, study or sunbathe on the green where shots were fired for freedom. In Portsmouth, people go about their daily lives. They shop in Market Square. They lace up sneakers and walk on their lunch hour. History happened here, and they're okay with it.

And the houses themselves are far from done. Lauren Gianino of the Moffatt-Ladd House points out that just a couple of years ago, someone found sheets of the original wallpaper in a closet.

"The house," she says, "is not done giving up its secrets."

Chapter 9

MANCHESTER AND NASHUA

THE MILLS

Jeffrey Barraclough, executive director of the Millyard Museum, is certain of one thing: Manchester as he and we know it today would not exist without the Amoskeag Mills. "It would," he says, "have remained a small town."

"The mills built the city," according to Barraclough.

The idea that would become New Hampshire's Queen City began in May 1807 with a canal and lock system devised by Samuel Blodgett in what was then known as Derryfield, a small farming community perched on the banks of the mighty Merrimack River. It would grow to become the home of the largest textile mill complex in the world and reinvent itself into a hub of technology, business and education.

Blodget envisioned a textile center similar, if not better than Manchester, England, then at the forefront of the Industrial Revolution. "Derryfield" was reborn as "Manchester" in 1810. In that same year, Benjamin Prichard and the three Stevens brothers, Ephraim, David and Robert, built a mill on the west bank of the Merrimack, where they had acquired the water rights the year before. The mill struggled, even with the development of new machinery in 1811. It passed into the hands of Dr. Oliver Dean, Lyman Tiffany and Willard Sayles of Massachusetts, and in April 1826, Dr. Dean supervised the construction of a new mill, the Bell Mill, named for the bell tower on the roof. A second mill, the Island Mill, was built on an island in the Merrimack.[44]

Based on the model in nearby Lowell, Massachusetts, boardinghouses and company stores sprang up within walking distance of the mills. The

Cloth from Manchester's Amoskeag Mills stretched around the world. *Library of Congress, Prints & Photographs Division, Farm Security Administration/Office of War Information Black-and-White Negatives, LC-USF342-013205-A [P&P] LOT 1222.*

Amoskeag Manufacturing Company incorporated on July 1, 1931. The corporate offices were established in Boston, with a local manager to oversee the day-to-day.

Manchester was a planned city, laid out in blocks and grids. "They wanted a city that was desirable to live in," according to Barraclough. The founders left ample room for parks, schools and churches.

Manchester was a company town from the beginning. Amoskeag's engineering branch built all the machinery for all the mills, promoting a consistency, and the red brick for its buildings came from the company brickyard in nearby Hooksett.

TENEMENTAL JOURNEY

The company provided everything they thought a worker would need, including six blocks of boardinghouses for workers at Stark Mill No. 1, completed in 1839. There were churches, hospitals, fire stations, a library and access to rail service. Parks provided outdoor recreation, and lecture halls and theaters provided indoor entertainment. Rows of tenements provided housing for working families, while mansions housed the managers.

The mills, and the town, flourished under Amoskeag's direction.

Though mill life was rigorous, it beat poverty. Young women from hill farms flocked to Manchester, the mills and the boardinghouses in spite of the especially strict standards for women: dress codes, curfews, morality clauses. One has to wonder what they were running away from. But they

Following the Lowell model, the Amoskeag Mills provided for every aspect of a worker's life, including housing. *Library of Congress, Prints & Photographs Division, Farm Security Administration/ Office of War Information Black-and-White Negatives, LC-USF342- 015584-A [P&P] LOT 1222.*

came. French Canadians left their farms for the short trip south and a better life, one that would include their becoming a major influence in the growing city. As the need for workers increased, Greeks, Poles, Swedes and Germans found their way west and then north. Partly for convenience's sake, partly by design, they huddled in ethnic enclaves with folks from home. Churches and small neighborhood markets fed their need for their own religion and their own food. The West Side of the river would eventually become a city within the city, occupied by French Canadians and steeped in their culture.

It was a hard life, just not as hard as the one most of them had left. But they worked it. By the mid-twentieth century, most of these immigrants would own houses and hold supervisory positions in the mills. Their offspring would work in the trades or the professions, and their names would appear on city boards and committees. By the twenty-first century, Manchester's welcome mat would expand to include people from Asia, Africa and Latin countries seeking that better life.

The mill complex, as seen from Canal Street. *Library of Congress, Prints & Photographs Division, HABS NH,6-MANCH,2-.*

But first they had to go through growing pains.

Amoskeag pivoted during the Civil War, with its foundry making muskets and carbines for the Union. In World War I, the complex provided the government with war materiel. The war was good to workers, who received both a raise and shorter hours. In 1911, the firm established the Amoskeag Textile Club, with everything from athletic teams to cultural events to a path to homeownership. There were visiting nurses, libraries and playgrounds.

But it wasn't enough to stop the tidal wave that was coming, a national recession and its successor, the Great Depression. In 1922, agent Parker Straw posted a notice mandating a 20 percent pay reduction, with hours increased from forty-eight to fifty-four hours a week.

Encouraged by the United Textile Workers of America, the Amoskeag millworkers held their first strike. It would last for nine months. While the pay cut was restored, the return to the forty-eight-hour week did not happen. The workers went back to their looms out of necessity, with only part of their demands met.

"They struggled with antiquated machinery, labor unrest," Barraclough notes.

By now, the workers knew the owners wouldn't save them. The paternalism and the "company town" mentality were gone forever.

And so was the North's dominance of the textile industry. The industry migrated to the South, where new equipment and lower labor costs made doing business more efficient. The South was to have its own struggles.[45]

Young women, some barely into their teens, found work at the Amoskeag Mills in Manchester. Child and teen labor was a way of life. *Library of Congress, Prints & Photographs Division, Farm Security Administration/Office of War Information Black-and-White Negatives, LC-103.*

Workers wait for the doors to open at one of the mills in the giant Amoskeag Mills complex. *Library of Congress, Prints & Photographs Division, Farm Security Administration/Office of War Information Black-and-White Negatives, LC-DIG-nclc-01799.*

The mill owners again attempted to cut pay and expand hours, resulting in violent strikes in 1933 and 1934. The New Hampshire State Militia, now the National Guard, was called on to intervene. The Amoskeag Manufacturing Company closed its doors and filed for bankruptcy on Christmas Eve 1935.

Around fifteen thousand people were out of work, according to Barraclough. That was one-third to one-half of the city's population. "There was a real fear," he says, "that it would become a ghost town." The winter of 1936 was "pretty dire" for the Queen City, and the flood in March 1936 made it worse. "The first floor of the mill buildings was completely under water," he says. "It was the 'final nail.'"

Or so they thought.

But a group of influential citizens weren't about to let Manchester die.

Amoskeag Industries was established in 1936 by local businesspeople to promote economic conditions in Manchester. Its stated purpose was to "buy the assets of the Amoskeag Manufacturing Company out of bankruptcy." The new coalition feared out-of-state interests coming in, and they wanted Manchester for Manchester.

Barraclough has heard it all before, and told it all, but his voice still holds wonder. "They raised $5 million in less than a month; it was all New Hampshire money," he marvels. The auction was halted, and Amoskeag Industries went to work. So did much of the city.

According to the company's website, thousands of jobs were saved by the leasing of equipment and facilities in the historic Millyard district. Fifty-four businesses were established within a year, including Pacific Mills, Chicopee Mills, Amoskeag Worsted Mills and Waumbec Mills.

Grenier Field was Manchester's airport during the twentieth century. It was replaced by the bustling Manchester-Boston Regional Airport. *Library of Congress, Prints and Photographs Division, Historic American Engineering Record, HAER NH, 6-MANCH, 13A-.*

SECOND MILL ERA

The action gave rise to a second mill era, when the sons and daughters of the first immigrants, along with a wave of new immigrants, found good jobs and a foothold in the city. Manchester thrived again, under the leadership of businesspeople such as May Gruber and her first husband, Saul Sidore. They established their Pandora company in the 1940s in New York and eventually moved it to Manchester.

In 1950, the couple bought a Millyard building for their growing knitwear business, Pandora Industries, and soon were turning out sixty thousand sweaters a week with one thousand workers. These were, if not the glory days, some okay days for the sons and daughters of those early millworkers. The boardinghouse and tenement system was gone, but it didn't matter, because Pandora and Waumbec and BeeBee Shoe paid enough for their workers to buy modest houses and later upgrade to better ones. There was no company store, but the new generation of millworkers found everything they needed on Elm Street.

After Sidore's death in 1964, Gruber took the helm at Pandora. It was unusual to see a woman running a business in the '60s, let alone a major manufacturing concern. Gruber gave back, supporting charities with Sidore and later her second husband, Sam Gruber. She and Gruber had a particular focus on music, establishing music programs in schools and the community. She was a lifelong Democrat who helped found the local chapter of League of Women Voters and the New Hampshire Civil Liberties Union.

The second mill era lasted until the latter part of the twentieth century, when it succumbed to outsourcing to China and Mexico. The North suffered. The South suffered. We all suffered. Urban renewal came to Manchester in 1969, demolished some of the smaller mill buildings and filled in the canals. Pandora, last of the textile manufacturers, closed for good in 1983, according to Barraclough.

But Manchester again refused to die. "Manchester," Barraclough says, "is a city that refused to give up."

Amoskeag Industries invested in several projects around the city. In addition, entrepreneur Dean Kamen saw the potential of the Millyard and began buying up buildings in the 1980s. Other companies such as Brady Sullivan and Jeremy Hitchcock's DYN invested in the former mills.

"Dean Kamen," Barraclough says, "had a vision for what the Millyard could be used for." Mixed-use zoning was required and passed, allowing the Millyard to have business, industry, entertainment and housing units.

Opposite, top: The Amoskeag Mill complex is still at the forefront of business and technology, housing tech start-ups, small businesses, restaurants and two colleges, including the University of New Hampshire–Manchester. *Kathleen Bailey*.

Opposite, bottom: Tenement housing created by the Amoskeag mill system has been revamped into modern apartments. *Kathleen Bailey*.

Above: Real estate giants Brady Sullivan purchased the Jefferson Mill and use it as their headquarters, as well as leasing space to other businesses. *Kathleen Bailey*.

The Millyard is now a bustling complex hosting restaurants, small businesses, tech start-ups, the Millyard Museum, University of New Hampshire and Franklin Pierce University and an arts colony. Kamen's SEE Science Center features a giant LEGO rendering of the mill complex.

And bringing it all back home, Kamen's 1850 Associates now own the Pandora Building. They've modernized it into a "green" building, with carpet made from recycled soda bottles, a rainwater collection system and rooftop solar panels. The complex houses Kamen's SEE Science Center— and the Millyard Museum.

One feels May Gruber would have approved.

THE LOST COLONY OF MONSON

New Hampshire's first inland colony wasn't a roaring success. In fact, it didn't make it to the Revolution. The village of Monson, settled in 1737, was disbanded and deserted shortly after 1770.

The land was originally part of Massachusetts and covered seventeen thousand acres. The original settlers bore names like Wallingford, Gould, Clarke, Bayley, Brown and two families of Nevinses. They farmed, operated businesses, grew fruitful and multiplied.

But in the end, Monson wasn't enough to hold them.

In 1741, borders were adjusted, and Monson became part of New Hampshire. The land-that-was-Monson is part of the present-day towns of Hollis, Brookline, Amherst and Milford. The town was chartered in 1746.

Several theories have been floated for the colony's disbanding, though none is accepted as final fact. Were the settlers fearful of the Native Americans? Doubtful. Did the harsh living get to them? Probably not; it was harsh everywhere. Were there political reasons? Maybe, although nobody knows what.

The land held its secrets for two hundred years. It was mostly undisturbed, although Clarke descendant Russell Dickerman lived nearby and kept an eye on the property. In 1998, a local developer wanted to put a twenty-eight-lot subdivision on the grounds. Dickerman and his wife, Geri, weren't having any. A coalition coalesced, consisting of the New Hampshire Division of Historic Resources, Inherit New Hampshire (now the New Hampshire Preservation Alliance), the Society for the Protection of New Hampshire Forests and random volunteers drawn in by the Dickermans. The Forest Society ended up purchasing most of the land, with the Dickermans donating another 125 acres they owned. The group raised $350,000 over six months, with four hundred major donors.

The complex now includes roads, fields, cellar holes with markers describing who lived there and one house, the Gould House, restored by Dickerman and used as a museum.

Matt Scaccia, community relations and recreation manager with the Forest Society, has made Monson his special project and put faces to the people who lived, laughed, loved and sometimes died in the houses above the cellar holes. For example, a Mr. Bayley lived just down the road from the Gould House, and he was a cobbler. "He would take his bench around to the different houses," Scaccia says. "He made house calls for shoes."

A crisp fall day in Monson, the abandoned village. *Sheila Bailey.*

Many of the male residents, including Thomas Nevins, served in the French and Indian War, according to Scaccia. "This was the Monson era," he says, adding, "Lexington and Concord came after." Thomas Nevins would lose three sons to the Revolution.

The physician, Dr. John Brown, was probably the wealthiest Monsonian, Scaccia said. His "chaise cart" or buggy was the envy of his neighbors. It

The restored cabin and museum at Monson Center. *Sheila Bailey.*

was small by modern standards, or even later standards, Scaccia notes. "It had two wheels, one seat and a cover."

While Brown's services were required outside of Monson, Scaccia isn't sure how the town could support Abijah Gould, a clockmaker. "They told time by the sun and seasons," he muses. Still, Gould's work survived. His son Abijah followed him into the clockmaking field, and at least one of his pieces is owned by the New Hampshire Historical Society.

The people of Monson never got around to building a school, town hall or any public building. The closest they came was a town pound for stray animals. But they did have a government, with selectmen, and they did pay taxes, then to Royal Governor Benning Wentworth.

Though the town gave up its charter, people continued to live in the homes, some into the 1800s. Others moved north, some to Hebron on the Cockermouth River, some to Plymouth. The cobbler Bayley's son lived in his old house until it burned down, "and then he went west with the Mormons," Scaccia says. Other houses burned one by one, never to be rebuilt.

Except for the houses, the village is "remarkably intact," according to Scaccia. The cellar holes are still there, the roads are still there. "It's remarkable to see," he notes.

The road to the Lost Village of Monson. *Courtesy Society for the Protection of New Hampshire Forests.*

The complex is significant archaeologically and has hosted a couple of digs, according to the Forest Society. But the artifacts recovered were "very scant," Scaccia adds. Monson's residents took most of their stuff with them. "There are some very old horseshoes, an old shoe or belt buckle, a handful of coins," he says. "It's remarkable that Dr. Brown's cart survived."

Dickerman and his father restored the Gould House to the best of their ability, using pieces from the original house. It was added onto in the 1840s, a time that seems like ancient history to us but was the "future" at the height of Monson.

And the restoration revealed treasures. "One of the things they found," Scaccia says, "was a template for making a violin." Apparently, Gould didn't just make clocks. "They found it in the walls," Scaccia marvels.

The names of most of the early settlers were obtained from a 1915 record book and used for plaques naming who lived where. "Others," Scaccia says, "lived on in people's heads."

Scaccia says, "I've worked on a lot of properties, but Monson has a unique feeling. It's one of the most serene places we operate. The fields are open, there are American chestnut trees, there's a beautiful heron rookery. I've seen over twenty blue herons."

Russ and Geri Dickerman partnered with the Society for the Protection of New Hampshire Forests to preserve his family's ancestral land and the lost village of Monson. *Courtesy Sophie Oehler/Society for the Protection of New Hampshire Forests.*

And though the village has been the focus of some paranormal investigators, that doesn't interest Scaccia. He already knows "his" people.

In addition to Forest Society staff, the village has a host of volunteers. Some work on the trails system, some maintain the gardens. A local farmer keeps the fields hayed. Dickerman visited the property daily until his health began to fail.[46]

The volunteers, and the Forest Society, have no plans to "improve" the site nor to abandon it. "Forever," Scaccia says, "is forever."

TAKING THEM *INTO* THE BALL GAME

They were one year ahead of Jackie Robinson, and they did it in New Hampshire.

Robinson's history-changing charge into Major League Baseball occurred on April 15, 1947, when he started at first base for the then Brooklyn Dodgers. The media-heavy debut was hailed as the end of racial segregation in professional baseball. The act brought the eventual end of the Negro League, an incubator for talented players since the 1880s.

But New Hampshire got there first. In 1946, Black players Roy Campanella and Don Newcombe quietly joined the minor-league club the Nashua Dodgers. The Dodgers were thus the first racially integrated professional baseball team in the United States. Catcher Campanella would eventually be inducted into the Baseball Hall of Fame, and Pitcher Newcombe would eventually win a Cy Young Award.

In the 1980s and '90s, Steve Daly was a young sportswriter and later assistant sports editor at the Nashua, New Hampshire *Telegraph*. He wrote a story for the paper on the Dodgers and their breakthrough. "But I did a little more digging and realized that this was a really important team in the history of integration," Daly says. "It deserved more than a seventy-inch story." The result of his "digging"? A book, *Dem Little Bums: The Nashua Dodgers*, published in 1993 by Plaidswede Publishers of Concord, New Hampshire.

The Nashua Dodgers were a farm team of the Brooklyn Dodgers. "Dem Little Bums" came from Brooklyn's affectionate moniker for its team, "Dem Bums."[47]

Pitcher Don Newcombe and Catcher Roy Campanella were the first baseball players to integrate a minor-league team, a year before Jackie Robinson integrated the Majors. They are commemorated with this mural in Nashua, New Hampshire, home of the former Nashua Dodgers. *Kathleen Bailey.*

Barbara Ward is Black and grew up in a family of sports fans. But the grant writer and education specialist for the Black Heritage Trail of New Hampshire didn't realize what had happened in Nashua until she was an adult. Like Daly, she knew these stories had to be told.

Ward says she's fascinated by how the Dodgers strategized to bring equity to the ballpark. "There was Jackie in Canada, playing for a AAA team," she says of the legendary Robinson. "And there were Don and Roy in Nashua, playing for a AA team. [Dodgers general manager] Branch Rickey really wanted them to come next."[48]

Rickey's strategizing included seeding Nashua with a pitcher and a catcher. These were critical roles, Ward explains: some White catchers didn't want to catch balls thrown by Black pitchers. "You can see what he was up against," she says of Rickey.

Campanella and Newcombe had already made headlines in the former Negro League, and Branch Rickey was determined to mine their talent. He first offered the pair to a Dodgers affiliate in Danville, Illinois, but was politely told that the heartland wasn't ready for integration.

In 1945, Rickey contacted executive Emil "Buzzie" Bavasi about finding a location for a new club in the reformed New England League, a club that would be open to players of any color. Rickey had just signed Jackie Robinson to play in Montreal for the International League, and Rickey knew integration was on its way. Bavasi scouted New England for a suitable location. He searched for a community with a significant French-Canadian population, believing they would be more accepting of blacks, and he found it in Nashua. Nashua was no stranger to professional baseball, having hosted teams since the turn of the century. This would be something different.

Nashua did have a significant population of French Canadians. But at the time of Campanella's and Newcombe's signings, there were fewer than fifty African Americans in the city.

They made it work.

At the time Daly wrote his book, several of the "Little Bums" were still alive. "I was able to talk with a bunch of them," he recalls, "and some of them were crying on the phone. They had such fond memories of Nashua."

With the exception of the two breakout stars, few of the Little Bums stayed in baseball. It's the way of the minor leagues, Daly muses: "It's a sobering experience. Nearly all the players are as good as you are." He characterizes the majority of the Nashua Dodgers as "lunch pail guys, not superstars in the making."

But the love of the game kept them in Nashua.

Nashua was a good gamble by Rickey and Bavasi. On the third day of the 1946 season, Newcombe claimed the victory over a Pawtucket, Rhode Island team, making him the first African American pitcher to win a game for an integrated professional baseball team.

In that first year, Campanella batted .291, hit 13 home runs and was named the team's MVP. Newcombe won fourteen games, lost four and had a 2.21 earned run average. Campanella also briefly managed the team in a game against Lynn, Massachusetts, becoming the first African American to manage an integrated professional baseball team. It looked random to outsiders, but Ward says that was also part of manager Walter Alston's strategy. There was some heckling, and it upset Alston, who then told Campanella, "I'm going to get myself kicked out. You're going to manage the rest of the game." Alston picked a fight and got tossed out, and Campanella took the helm.

Oh, and they won the game.

Their personal victories were as important as their professional ones. Newcombe stayed with a White family during his stint in Nashua, sleeping in one of their beds and eating at their table. Most of the players boarded with families, Daly points out, because they were paid very little. A White auto dealer gave Newcombe his first car, and a White barber attempted to cut their hair. The result, according to Daly, was "brutal," especially for Newcombe. "They had a game that night, and people laughed at his haircut," Daly recalls. "But that was okay. He laughed it off. The cheers from the fans were what mattered."

Nashua was also a relatively small town for the pair, according to Daly. He points out, "Don was from Elizabeth, New Jersey, and Roy was from Philadelphia. They were way out of their element."

There were no racial incidents in Nashua, according to their firsthand accounts, and only one serious one on the road in a game with a Lynn, Massachusetts team, the same game Campanella ended up managing. "Nashua was a melting pot," Daly points out. "There were so many people from different backgrounds, having to pay their dues. The town was very welcoming."

Technically, Robinson had already integrated pro baseball, due to his stint in Montreal. But that was with the International League, Daly points out, and a Triple-A team. Brooklyn was what counted. In 1947, the pressure was on for Robinson, whom Rickey had chosen for his cool and control. "Jackie," Daly says, "represented an entire race. And Jackie could turn his cheek."

Rickey initially considered Newcombe too volatile for integrating a team. Daly remembers a conversation with Newcombe. "Branch told him, 'There is no way I'll be able to use you. You couldn't handle the pressure.'" But Newcombe surprised him, and Nashua surprised everyone.

Officially, Newcombe and Campanella didn't suffer the harassment Robinson underwent. For one thing, their profile was lower. Nobody was about to put a Nashua team in *Life* magazine. For another, Bavasi and general manager Walter Alston had their own fists cocked to protect their guys. And they had something worth protecting.

Michael Atkins, an attorney and Executive Council member of the Greater Nashua NAACP, notes, "Certainly, the fact Don and Roy were in the minors would likewise have contributed to the difference in the amount of attention that the respective signing(s) and assignments garnered. Also, the community in Nashua NH simply embraced and welcomed both Don and Roy." When Newcombe came back to Nashua for a visit in the mid-1990s, he talked about how appreciative he was and how welcome he felt in Nashua, according to Atkins.

This plaque on Nashua's Holman Stadium commemorates the Nashua Dodgers, the first minor-league baseball team to be integrated. *Kathleen Bailey.*

Nashua's historic Holman Stadium continues to host baseball, currently with the Silver Knights minor-league team. *Kathleen Bailey.*

Was it really a field of dreams? Ward has her doubts. "I'm sure," she says, "that there were some incidents. But they didn't talk about them."

Newcombe would go on to be a four-time All Star, winning the Cy Young and the National League MVP. Campanella set major-league records for catchers, with 41 homers and 142 RBIs in 1953.

A plaque was hung on Holman Stadium on May 30, 2023, marking it as part of the Black Heritage Trail of New Hampshire.[49] The stadium already had banners supporting Newcombe's and Campanella's achievements, their numbers and Robinson's hung inside, and access streets are named in their honor.

What does this say about Newcombe and Campanella? Atkins thinks that their success in the frozen North speaks to the character of both men. Atkins notes, "They were amongst the very first to reintegrate professional baseball, and they, like Jackie and those that followed, carried the extra weight of not only making it for themselves and their families but also for all of those players they knew may be able to follow them from the Negro Leagues into MLB. Certainly there was very little, if any, margin for error for them both on and off the field. They carried that 'extra weight' with dignity, class and success."

What does this say about the Granite State, which was whiter-than-white in the late 1940s and isn't much darker now? It says that when the rest of the country is patting itself on the back, we've most likely already done it. We started the Revolution, Paul Revere and all, in December 1774.[50] When the "18th of April, 75" arrived, we had already seized a fort and thrown out a royal governor. In Manchester, a woman headed a major corporation well before feminism. We don't talk about it; we just do it.

Chapter 10

SACRED SPACES

THE LEGACY OF BUD THOMPSON

Charles "Bud" Thompson arrived in New Hampshire with a guitar on his back and songs to sing. He left New Hampshire, and this world, as the founder of one museum and the change agent for another.

Thompson was born on April 12, 1922, of strong German and Scottish stock. His paternal grandmother, a native of Prussia, provided piety and pacifism. His grandfather Alexander Thompson had only an eighth-grade education. But with native intelligence and grit, he became an executive with a leading producer of men's suits. He also developed the "Thompsonian method" of sales, designed to take the pressure off customers. Alexander also developed a taste for opera and taught himself Italian.

Young Charles moved a dozen to thirteen times in his childhood, due to his father's work. In second grade, the family landed in Rhode Island, and young Bud had an experience that would mark his life. The class had a special visitor, Chief Sachem Silver Star of the Pequot tribe. He explained the Native way of life, including how the seasons move in a circle and the earth orbits the sun, and told them they were all part of the circle of life. He further told them that the Great Spirit gave each child a special gift to use to make the world better and that it was their responsibility to find it and use it.

"That talk," Bud's son Darryl says, "changed Dad's life."[51]

Thompson developed an interest in Native American lore, legend, craft and life. He wrote a letter to Silver Star, who answered it, "and he kept it all his life," Darryl Thompson says. Bud also developed an interest in plants

Today's Canterbury Shaker Village looks much as it did in this 1960s photo. *Alfred Perron.*

and herbs, which would serve him well in his work with both Shakers and Native Americans.

If Thompson wanted to do something, he learned it. He took up guitar and, at sixteen, had a fifteen-minute radio show, *The Singing Cowboy*. He later learned opera and performed as an extra with the Metropolitan Opera in New York City.

"He had tremendous self-confidence," Darryl Thompson says, adding, "And he knew how to reinvent himself."

Bud Thompson quit high school with only two classes left, "a decision he would regret the rest of his life," according to Darryl. He wanted to serve his country at the outbreak of World War II. He joined the Merchant Marine and served stateside. He sang in churches and bonded with a young woman, Harriet Waller, a church organist, whom he soon married.

And he was to reinvent himself one more time, as a traveling folk singer. The country was in the grips of a folk revival, and so-called song collectors were touring remote regions to find and record forgotten tunes. Thompson worked summers at the Arnold Arboretum in Jamaica Plain, Massachusetts, and toured the country as a folk singer in autumn, winter and spring. He toured the Midwest searching for songs but found the heartland "picked clean," according to his son.

An executive at Thompson's booking agency, Lordly and Dunn, said, "What about the music of the American Utopias?"

"Dad looked at him and said, 'What's a utopia?'" Darryl Thompson recalls.

HANDS TO WORK, HEARTS TO GOD

To anyone from the outside, the Shaker religion often seems a daunting prospect. Living communally, working for the common good, burying all desire for personal property and advancement—oh, and did we mention celibacy?

But the practice of the faith lasted in New Hampshire for almost two hundred years, and its legacy lives on in a quiet part of Canterbury.

The faith had its roots in England, when dissenters from various religions such as Quakers and Methodists formed a new religion based on prophecy. Their visions resulted in ecstasies and dance, which earned them the nickname "Shakers," for "Shaking Quakers." Their official title was the United Society of Believers in Christ's Second Appearing.

Though James and Jane Wardley founded the sect in 1747, "Mother" Ann Lee's charismatic personality was responsible for its growth. She called her followers to confession of sins, relinquishment of worldly goods and, in particular, abstinence from sex and all "lustful gratifications." The group practiced celibacy and communal child-rearing. Men and women lived separately but were equal.

Under Lee's leadership, the Shakers immigrated to America in 1774. Her husband, Abraham Stanley, joined her on the trip but left her once he was in the States and eventually remarried. This didn't daunt Lee and her followers. Nor were they daunted when, in Watervliet, New York, they were briefly jailed for refusing to sign an Oath of Allegiance to their new country. They eventually established nineteen colonies from Maine to Kentucky. It didn't hurt that Lee billed herself as the Second Coming of Christ.

The Canterbury group was established in 1792 and remained a home for Shakers until the last living Canterbury Shaker, Sister Ethel Hudson, died in 1992.

The Canterbury Shakers reached their peak in the 1850s, when three hundred people lived and worked in more than one hundred buildings. They farmed three thousand acres. They developed new species of fruits, vegetables and herbs. In their spare time, they tinkered, looking for better ways to do things. Shakers invented the clothespin, the circular saw and an early version of the washing machine.

Canterbury Shakers were aggressive entrepreneurs, selling their goods in nearby Concord or to people who came to them. They reinvested their funds in the property, and by the mid-nineteenth century, they were wealthy. They also reinvested their profits in charitable endeavors.

The sexes were strictly separated, to the point of separate entrances into buildings. The Shakers managed to perpetrate themselves when women or couples with children joined. The children were taken from their parents and "raised" by the Shakers. The Shakers also took in orphans and raised and educated them.

Thompson researched the Shaker music, after looking up utopias in general, and found that they had more than ten thousand songs. "They never said 'composed,' they said they 'received' the songs," Darryl Thompson notes. A friend at the Thompsons' church had produced a silent movie about the Shakers, and Thompson was immediately intrigued. He wrote to the three surviving Shaker villages in New England: Hancock, Massachusetts; Sabbathday Lake, Maine; and Canterbury, New Hampshire. He eventually traveled to Canterbury, with the aim of obtaining songs for his book.

It didn't go quite the way he planned.

In Canterbury, he found fourteen Shaker sisters trying to keep the complex going. They had three gift shops, selling everything from Shaker antiques to rummage. They also gave tours of the complex, a practice that had been common since the 1850s. They needed the money, and they figured the tours were a way to fend off misconceptions about their way of life.

But by the 1950s, the remaining sisters were aging. They told Thompson they were thinking about giving up the tours. They already had tours

Opposite: Eldress Bertha Lindsay, then Sister Bertha, works a loom producing poplarware in the late 1950s. *Alfred Perron*.

Left: The clean lines of Shaker furniture span the centuries and makes it popular with collectors. *Alfred Perron*.

Below: This room-length cupboard shows the functionality of Shaker design. *Alfred Perron*.

booked for the summer and asked if he would conduct them. That was the summer of 1957.

They never closed.

Thompson fell in love with the Shakers, if not the way of life, and stayed on as their handyman, tour guide and general factotum. He saw the potential of the complex and began grooming it for a museum, where the peaceful but industrious way of life could be interpreted for future generations. He restored buildings, managed the public profile and cared for the remaining sisters as though they were his own aunts.

Harriet and son Darryl (born in 1957) moved onto the property in 1959, and son Dayne was born in 1961. Darryl Thompson grew up with fourteen grandmothers.

"It was wonderful," he recalls. When his mother worked as a music teacher, the sisters provided childcare. When they were baking, they offered him a little rolling pin; when they were gardening, they gave him a little trowel. The acres of fields and stone walls gave two little boys unlimited capacity for adventure.

"The sisters," he says, "loved children." When his father married Nancy Erickson Lamb, his second wife, the sisters equally embraced his stepbrothers, Stephen and David Lamb. The families became part of the Shaker family, in good times and bad.

Darryl's father had a vision for the village. He knew it could be so much more, and he began a campaign to convince the sisters to make it into a living history museum. He took Eldress Bertha Lindsay, Sister Lillian Phelps and Sister Marguerite Frost to places like Sturbridge Village and Shelburne, Vermont. The revived and restored Canterbury Shaker Village opened to the public in 1960.

And an itinerant singer with no diploma had gotten them there.

What motivated a young man with no museum background to put all his energies behind an undertaking like this? It goes back to Chief Silver Star and using one's gifts, Darryl Thompson believes.

Opposite: Eldress Gertrude Soule chats with a representative of a Native American tribe during a powwow. Charles "Bud" Thompson brought two of his passions, Shakers and Native culture, together on a regular basis. *Alfred Perron.*

Above, from left: Eldress Bertha Lindsay, Sister Miriam Wall and Eldress Gertrude Soule participate in the 200th anniversary celebration of the Shakers' arrival in America. The celebration was held in August 1974. *Alfred Perron.*

Left: Eldress Bertha Lindsay makes remarks during the 200th anniversary of the Shakers' arrival in America. *Alfred Perron.*

"My father," he says, "was inspired by the Shakers. He was interested in how God used ordinary people to do extraordinary things."

Thompson was with the remaining Shakers until the end.

The Shakers had less education than Bud Thompson: their village school went only to the eighth grade. But they tapped their potential and the potential of the community to make a dizzying difference in the world. Beyond the clothespin, they influenced both the American garden seed industry as the first to package and sell seeds and the pharmaceutical industry with their knowledge of herbs. They promoted equal rights for women and minorities. Then there's the furniture, which inspired both Scandinavian design and the Arts and Crafts movement.

Opposite: Charles "Bud" Thompson was with his Shakers in all seasons of life. *Alfred Perron.*

Above: In keeping with their communal nature, the Canterbury Shakers had one gravestone. *Alfred Perron.*

Right: Eldress Bertha Lindsey was the public face of the Canterbury Shakers in their last years. *Alfred Perron.*

Opposite, top: A wistful winter night at the Canterbury Shaker Village. *Sheila Bailey.*

Opposite, bottom: A winter landscape at Canterbury Shaker Village. *Sheila Bailey.*

Above: Luminarias light the way in a winter dusk at Canterbury Shaker Village. *Sheila Bailey.*

Though the sisters are gone, and the brothers have been gone for a while, their lifestyle and legacy live on. It's a little more formal than when Thompson gave the tours and his boys ran around in the meadow, but the spirit of the place, and its dwellers, remains.

The museum is now a 501(c)(3) nonprofit. Visitors can see twenty-five original Shaker buildings. These include the original Meetinghouse and Dwelling House, both on their original sites. The property is under conservation easement. The museum is open for guided tours, self-guided tours and events such as summer concerts and Merry, Merry Canterbury in December.

But it is arguably best appreciated on a crisp fall or frigid winter evening, when leaves or snow muffle the footfalls and lamplight beckons from the ancient windows.

COMING HOME TO KEARSARGE

Bud Thompson never forgot his original dream, the dream to honor Native American life in all its fullness. Thompson began his own collection of artifacts, with a goal of starting an Indian museum, while still living with the Shakers. His second wife, Nancy, shared his vision.

Ironically, Darryl Thompson says, as with the folk songs, his father didn't find the best pickings in the West. He found them in New England, tucked away in attics and cellars of people whose ancestors had brought them home from the West as souvenirs. Some he was able to buy outright, while others he purchased on installment from friendly dealers.

Today, the Mount Kearsarge Indian Museum (MKIM) brims with baskets, pottery and beaded creations. A slideshow in the spacious foyer highlights the work of Indigenous craftspeople. Exhibits highlight every major Native American group in America, from Abenaki to Seminole to Plains. A museum shop offers curated gifts, and a short film highlights the collection—and the collector.

It wasn't always this way.

This structure, formerly an indoor riding arena, became the fulfilment of one couple's dream as the Mount Kearsarge Indian Museum. *Sheila Bailey.*

Andrew Bullock, a longtime friend of Thompson's, remembers visiting him one summer day. Thompson was still running the Shaker complex in Canterbury, and he told Bullock, "Let's go for a ride." They motored over to Warner, a small town on the other side of Concord, and began the ascent that would eventually lead to Mount Kearsarge. But they stopped on a rustic property with a glorious view and not much else. The building Thompson led Bullock to wasn't promising. It was still being used as an indoor riding arena, Bullock recalls, with wood chips on the floors and pigeons nesting in the rafters.

What did he think? Bullock shrugs. "By that time, I'd known Bud fifteen years. If he put his mind to something, I knew it was going to happen."

Bullock, current director of the MKIM, grew up in a family with Native American roots. His parents attended powwows, and the young Bullock became fascinated with the Indian way of life. He met Thompson as a teen and vividly remembers his first meeting. "There was this man with a wide straw hat, and he had an elderly woman on each elbow." Thompson had brought two of his Shakers to experience Native life. He and the young Bullock found a mutual interest in Native American art, and Bullock began to hang out in Canterbury.

"The highlight of every visit," he recalls, "was going up on the second floor of the schoolhouse." Thompson kept his growing Native American collection there. "I would *ooh* and *aah* over his collection," Bullock says.

Bullock stayed in touch with Thompson when he went off to Trent University in Ontario, Canada, and majored in Native studies and anthropology. He continued his visits to Canterbury and watched Thompson's growing accumulation. Though Thompson didn't yet have a building, he had sorted his finds according to where they would go. "He'd say, 'This is the horse collection. This is the Plains Indian collection.'"

The Thompsons bought property in Warner, near the ascent to Mount Kearsarge, and began to plan. Like-minded people gathered around them. They conceived the museum not only to preserve Native culture but also to promote the environment.

They saw their dream become reality in 1991. Bud was seventy years of age. The initial displays were relatively sparse, comprising only the Thompsons' items. Bud and Nancy ran the facility themselves, with Bud giving the tours. Bullock was on the first board of trustees. When the museum incorporated as a 501(c)(3), they began to receive both financial donations and artifacts.

Bullock stayed involved as a trustee and "on most of the committees," he says. He became director in 2017.

This tepee is part of the outdoor attractions at the Mount Kearsarge Indian Museum. *Sheila Bailey.*

"The collection is remarkable," he says of the resources accumulated by MKIM. But, Bullock warns, there's more to this museum than stuff on a shelf. Thompson saw a bigger picture.

"One of the things that brought him here," Bullock says, "was the twelve acres of land." Thompson had an intense interest in the environment. "Early on, he was interested and concerned about the world we would leave the next generation." With MKIM, Bullock says, his mentor wanted to show where things came from and connect them to the larger world. Birch trees on the property would be fashioned into canoes, ash splints woven into baskets. "He never wanted the biggest pottery collection, the biggest artifact collection."

The Medicine Woods is another example of Thompson's philosophy. It covers two or three acres, according to Bullock. The space is planted with herbs the Native people would have used for healing. Thompson was the chief architect of the woods. "Virtually all the rocks on the paths, he put in place," Bullock marvels. In his later years, Thompson still spent time weeding and cultivating the herbs.

Ironically, Bullock says, "It's where the farm's 'dump' had been. He had to go in and remove tractor parts and the like."

The Medicine Woods was a special project of the Mount Kearsarge Indian Museum's founder, Charles "Bud" Thompson. *Sheila Bailey.*

Bud Thompson tends to flowers outside the Mount Kearsarge Indian Museum. *Collection photograph used by permission of Mount Kearsarge Indian Museum.*

Left: An Apache olla basket, part of the collection at the Mount Kearsarge Indian Museum in Warner. *Collection photograph used by permission of Mount Kearsarge Indian Museum.*

Below: Andrew Bullock, current director of the Mount Kearsarge Indian Museum, takes a break outside the main building. *Sheila Bailey.*

Opposite: Bud Thompson gives an acceptance speech for his Profile Award in May 2008 as his wife, Nancy, looks on. *Collection photograph used by permission of Mount Kearsarge Indian Museum.*

Thompson put up signs for each medicinal plant, which included its common name and its Latin name. He lined the paths with inspirational quotes about land stewardship. The signs have faded, according to Bullock, and an upcoming project will be renewing them and including the herbs' Native names.

"Every museum is different in its own way," Bullock muses. He has two concepts he'd like to see visitors take away, and they're not too different from the founder's. "One, we'd like people to realize that Native people are alive and well and living in New Hampshire," he says. "This is *their* story."

He'd also like his guests to experience the breadth and depth of Native culture, observing, "The museum is broken down into seven different galleries across North America. Bud's vision was that Native Americans weren't just one monolithic group." The Pequot museum in Connecticut focuses on the Pequot experience, while Plimoth Plantation focuses on the Wampanoags. MKIM honors every tribe and every nation.

Since its opening, MKIM has hosted visitors from all over the United States, thirty-eight foreign countries and countless school trips. Thompson

Bud Thompson gives an early tour at the Mount Kearsarge Indian Museum. *Collection photograph used by permission of Mount Kearsarge Indian Museum.*

lived to be ninety-nine, visiting or phoning the museum every day. He even received his high school diploma from Kearsarge Regional High School. He also received a Profile Award for his contributions to the State of New Hampshire.

The museum is open for guided tours, self-guided tours and special events, including powwows, an Herb and Garden Day and the Kearsarge Maple Weekend, where visitors can see how the Native Americans harvested this precious liquid. The last powwow drew 3,500 people, according to Bullock.

Bullock and his current board are always seeking ways to be involved in the community and partner with other groups. Recently, they teamed up with the McAuliffe/Shepard Planetarium in Concord for a night of star-watching on MKIM's open fields. The planetarium provided the telescopes, MKIM the space for viewing. Bullock remembers one ten-year-old boy who came up to him with the observation, "I've never been outside in the dark."

"We give them a reason," Bullock says, "to be outside in the dark."

Thompson died in 2021, but both his legacies live on. Could an itinerant folk singer and high school dropout have preserved two ancient ways of life anywhere else? Maybe. Probably. But we're glad he did it here.

HOW TO GET THERE

Few attractions speak to New Hampshire quirkiness more than the Chicken Farmer sign on Route 103 in Newbury. Local legend claims that the sign originally read "Chicken Farmer, I Love You," and that it was painted in the '70s or '80s by a shy teenage boy in honor of the girl who lived on a chicken farm. There's no record as to whether the boy crossed the road to find true love. But the town of Newbury didn't mess with the sentiment, honoring eternal love to the best of its ability, which included clearing brush away from the declaration and furtive locals repainting the letters from time to time. In 2011, a resident complained about the "graffiti," and the Department of Transportation painted over it. However, the memory of young love was stronger, and an unknown resident repainted the missive. That was that, and the townspeople signed a petition to have the sign remain.

New Hampshire loves quirky, and nothing says "quirk" quite as much as the iconic Chicken Farmer sign on Route 103. *Kathleen Bailey.*

The New Hampshire spirit shines through Chicken Farmer and the other venues explored in this book. Here's how to get there:[52]

NORTH OF THE NOTCHES

BERLIN HISTORICAL SOCIETY, 119 High Street, Berlin 03570. Tuesday, Wednesday and Saturday, noon to 4:00 p.m., or by appointment. (603) 752-4590, www.berlinhistoricalsociety.org, berlinnhhistory@weebly.com

BETHLEHEM HERITAGE SOCIETY, 2182 Main Street, Bethlehem 03574. Call for hours. (603) 869-3330, Bethlehemheritagenh.org, visit@discoverbethlehemnh.org

THE ROCKS, 113 Glessner Road, Bethlehem 03574. The Carriage Barn at The Rocks is open to visitors on Tuesdays and Wednesdays from 1:00 to 3:00 p.m., restrooms inside the Carriage Barn open to the public daily from 10:00 a.m. to 4:00 p.m. (603) 444-6228, info@therocks.org

THE WHITE MOUNTAINS

THE OLD MAN/PROFILER PLAZA. Head up I-93 from Concord. Take Exit 34-B in Franconia Notch. Turn toward Aerial Tramway and take first left. Follow road to parking lot.

THE INDIAN HEAD. Best viewed from Indian Head Resort, 664 US Route 3, Lincoln, NH 03251.

THE OLD WOMAN/WATCHER. Go up Route 93 to the Cannon Mountain Tramway. Walk under the bridge and turn left at the Greenleaf Trail. Take smaller trail to side marked by a cairn. Follow trail to the Eaglet, a spire of rock resembling, well, a baby eagle. Follow trail past Eaglet. Watch out for falling rocks. Walk to edge of ridge and view the Watcher. Be careful going back.

LITTLETON HISTORICAL SOCIETY, 4 Union Street, Littleton. Open 10:00 a.m. to 3:00 p.m., Wednesdays and Saturdays. (603) 444-6435, lhistoricalsociety@gmail.com

LAKES REGION

Castle in the Clouds (Lucknow Estate), 455 Old Mountain Road, Moultonborough. May through October, 10:00 a.m. to 4:00 p.m. $20 adult, $15 senior (65-plus), $13 veteran (plus five family members at same rate), $10 child, five to seventeen, free to four and under. (603) 476-5900, info@castleintheclouds.org, www.castleintheclouds.org

Belknap Mill Museum, 25 Beacon Street East, Laconia. Open year-round, Tuesday through Friday, 9:00 a.m. to 5:00 p.m., Saturday from 9:00 a.m. to 1:00 p.m. (603) 524-8813, www.belknapmill.org

Weirs Beach, Lakeside Avenue, Laconia. www.weirsbeach.com

Chaos and Kindness Store, CAKE Theatre, 12 Veterans Square, Laconia. (603) 677-6360

UPPER VALLEY/DARTMOUTH–LAKE SUNAPEE

Saint-Gaudens National Historic Site, 139 Saint-Gaudens Road, Cornish. Open Memorial Day weekend through late October, 9:00 a.m. to 4:30 p.m. $10 entry fee. (603) 675-2175, www.nps.gov

The Fells, 456 NH Route 103-A, Newbury. Summer, Wednesday through Sunday, June 14–Labor Day Weekend, 10:00 a.m. to 4:00 p.m. Main house closed Mondays and Tuesdays. Fall, Saturdays, Sundays and Mondays, Labor Day through Columbus Day, 10:00 a.m. to 4:00 p.m. Main house open: $10 adults, $8 seniors and students six to seventeen, free to five and under. Family rate, two adults, two or more children, $25. When main house closed, $8 adults, $6 seniors/students, $3 children, $15 family rate. Winters, $5 per family. Always free to veteran and active military. (603) 763-4789, www.thefells.org

MONADNOCK REGION

HISTORIC HARRISVILLE, PO Box 79, Harrisville NH 03450. (603) 827-3722, historicharrisville@msn.com

MADAME SHERRI SITE, FOREST SOCIETY. (603) 225-9945, www.forestsociety.org, info@forestsociety.org

MADAME SHERRI SITE, CHESTERFIELD HISTORICAL SOCIETY. (603) 256-6727, chesterfieldhistoricalsociety@gmail.com

AT HOME WITH THE PRESIDENT

THE PIERCE HOMESTEAD, 301 2nd NH Turnpike, Hillsborough, New Hampshire. Open Memorial Day weekend through Columbus Day, summer hours Friday through Tuesday, 10:00 a.m. to 4:00 p.m., Saturday and Sunday, 11:00 a.m. to 4:00 p.m. Last tour at 3:00 p.m. September 9 and 10 through Columbus Day, Saturday and Sunday, 10:00 a.m. to 4:00 p.m. New Hampshire residents $4 ages eighteen to sixty-four, free to sixty-five and over; $3 ages six to seventeen, free to five and under. (603) 478-3165, www.nhstateparks.org

THE PIERCE MANSE, 14 Horseshoe Pond Lane, Concord. Memorial Day weekend through late October, guided tours, Thursday, Friday and Saturday, 10:00 a.m. to 3:00 p.m., also by appointment with three days' notice. $10 adults, $9 seniors, $5 children, $35 family rate. (603) 225-4555, www.piercemanse.org

THE HOMES OF PORTSMOUTH

THE WARNER HOUSE, 150 Daniel Street, Portsmouth. May 25–October 15, Thursday through Saturday, 11:00 a.m. to 4:00 p.m. $10 adults, $8 seniors. (603) 436-5909, www.warnerhoue.org

MOFFATT-LADD HOUSE, 154 Market Street, Portsmouth. Through October 15, Thursday through Tuesday, 11:00 a.m. to 4:00 p.m., $10 adults, $8 seniors. (603) 436-8221, director@moffattladd.org

Wentworth-Gardner House, 50 Mechanic Street, Portsmouth. Through October 12, Friday through Monday, 11:00 a.m. to 4:00 p.m. $8 adults. (603) 436-4406, housemanager@wentworth-gardner.org

MANCHESTER

Millyard Museum, 200 Bedford Street, corner of Commercial and Pleasant Streets, Manchester. Tuesday through Saturday, 10:00 a.m. to 4:00 p.m. (603) 622-7531

MONSON

Forest Society. (603) 225-9945, info@forestsociety.org, www.forestsociety.org

NASHUA

Nashua Dodgers mural, 31 West Hollis Street, Nashua.

Holman Stadium, 67 Amherst Street. City Rec Department. (603) 589-3370

LEGACY OF BUD THOMPSON

Shaker Village, 288 Shaker Road, Canterbury. Guided tours Tuesday through Sunday, 11:00 a.m. and 1:00 p.m., $25 admission. (603) 783- 9511, www.shakers.org

Mount Kearsarge Indian Museum, 18 Highlawn Road, Warner. Guided tours Monday through Saturday, 10:30 a.m. and 1:30 p.m., Sundays 1:30 p.m. $11 adults, $10 seniors. (603) 456-2600, info@indianmuseum.org

CHICKEN FARMER SIGN

From the east, sign is on the right side of Route 103, 4.3 miles from the intersection of Routes 103 and 114. From the left, sign is on the left about 2.1 miles from the Newbury Town Lake Sunapee beach landing.

MUSEUM TRAIL

THE NEW HAMPSHIRE HERITAGE MUSEUM TRAIL features several of the facilities discussed in this book: the Belknap Mill, Castle in the Clouds, Canterbury Shaker Village, the Millyard Museum, the Mount Kearsarge Indian Museum and the Moffatt-Ladd House. For more information, visit www.nhmuseumtrail.org.

BLACK HERITAGE TRAIL

On May 21, 1796, Ona Maria Judge Staines left the Philadelphia home of George and Martha Washington. She boarded a ship and ended up in Portsmouth, where she lived the rest of her life. Per executive order of Governor Chris Sununu, May 21 is Ona Judge Day in New Hampshire. Her story is one of those promoted by the Black Heritage Trail of New Hampshire. The trail started as the Portsmouth Black Heritage Trail but expanded as more stories of Black people's New Hampshire lives were discovered. The trail flowed out of the Seacoast to tell stories such as those of Don Newcombe and Roy Campanella. Still based in Portsmouth, the organization offers events, guided tours, a poetry series, a Black New England conference, a Juneteenth celebration and more.

FAIRS, FESTIVALS
AND THINGS TO DO

EXETER: UFO Festival, Labor Day Weekend, downtown. The Incident at Exeter hearkens back to September 3, 1965, when eighteen-year-old Norman Muscarello said he saw an alien spacecraft over a field in nearby Kensington. The historic, brass-plated town gets a chance to go cheeky with a trolley ride to the incident site, an alien pet costume contest and parade, kids' crafts and activities and speakers on the paranormal. www.exeterufofestival.org

FRANCONIA NOTCH: The New England Ski Museum. Established 1982 in Franconia Notch, with an Eastern Slope branch established in 2018 in North Conway. Collections include 17,000 volumes, 390 periodicals, 490 posters, 2,500 reels of film and 735 pairs of skis. Franconia Notch, (603) 823-7177; North Conway, (603) 730-5044. www.newenglandskimuseum.org

GOFFSTOWN: Giant Pumpkin Weigh-In and Regatta. Sponsored by the Goffstown Main Street Program, this event, usually the third weekend of October, has crafts, vendors, contests and, on Sunday afternoon, the chance to see community members ride down the Piscataquog River in costume and in hollowed-out giant pumpkins. Sponsored by the Goffsotwn Main Street Program. (603) 497-9933, info@goffstownmainstreet.org

LACONIA/WEIRS: Motorcycle Week. The Lakes Region is home to the oldest motorcycle rally in America, begun in 1916 when a so-called gypsy tour stopped on the southern shores of Lake Winnipesaukee. The rally was sanctioned the following year by the Federation of American Motorcyclists

(FAM), and rallies were held every summer, drawing motorcyclists from around the country. In 1938, the popular Hill Climb was established in Gilford. The rally increased from a weekend to a full week, wrapping around Father's Day. In 1964, the Hill Climb moved to Bryer Motorsports Park in Loudon, later to become the New Hampshire International Speedway. And the bikers still came, including the Hell's Angels. A riot between Angels and local police in 1965 tarnished the image of Bike Week, cutting it to three days. In the 1990s, Laconia and the FAM gradually brought the rally back to a full week and then the current nine days. The event is more family-friendly now. For more information, visit www.laconiamcweekend.com.

WARNER: Warner boasts five museums. In addition to the Mount Kearsarge Indian Museum, spend a day visiting the Nature Discovery Center, also on the grounds of Mount Kearsarge Museum (nhdcnh.org). Visit the Upton-Chandler House of the Warner Historical Society. And stop at 1 Depot Street to see the Warner Firefighters Museum, which shares space with the New Hampshire Telephone Museum. The phone museum bills itself as a "Tangible History of Communication," with docents ready to talk on subjects such as the "race to the patent office" and the undertaker who invented the dial system. The museum is based on the collections of the Violette and Bartlett families, who were active in twentieth-century communications, and also items from Gary Mitchell of Connecticut. May 1–October 31, Tuesday through Saturday, 10:00 a.m. to 4:00 p.m.; December, March and April, Tuesday and Saturday, 10:00 a.m. to 4:00 p.m. $9 adults, $7 seniors, $6 students K–12, $8 groups. (603) 456-2234

WINCHESTER: The Pickle Festival. Last Saturday of September, all day downtown. Gift shop, canning contest, pickle-eating contest, live music, farmers' market, vendors. www.winchesternhpicklefestival.org

NOTES

Chapter 1

1. Dr. Linda Upham-Bornstein, Discover Berlin, www.berlinnh.gov/discover-berlin.
2. Ibid.
3. Ibid.
4. Ibid.
5. Discover Berlin, www.berlinnh.gov.
6. New Hampshire Department of Correctionswww.corrections.nh.gov.

Chapter 2

7. Bethlehem, NH, www.bethlehemnh.org.
8. Ibid.
9. Ruth Pactor, "They Came to Breathe," courtesy Michael Dickerman, *Bethlehem, New Hampshire, 1999 Bicentennial Edition* (Bondcliff Books, 1999).
10. Ibid.
11. Bethlehem Historical Society, www.bethlehemhistoricalnh.org.
12. Sarah Masor, "National Hay Fever Relief Association," *Bethlehem, New Hampshire.*
13. Forest Society of New Hampshire, www.forestsociety.org.

Chapter 3

14. Western White Mountains, www.westernwhitemountains.com.
15. New Hampshire Department of Environmental Services.
16. Ibid.
17. Ibid.
18. 2020 census.
19. Littleton Area Historical Museum, littletonnhmuseum.com.
20. Harmony Park is open spring, summer and fall from 10:00 a.m. to 8:00 p.m. and is free.
21. It's in the *Guinness Book of World Records*. I do not make these things up.
22. By the late New Hampshire sculptor Emile Birch and funded by the Eames family.
23. GoLittleton, golittleton.com.

Chapter 4

24. See appendix II.
25. Adam Drapcho, "He's With the Band," *Laconia Daily Sun*, February 5, 2020.
26. Adam Drapcho, "Roy Small, Stroke Survivor Turned Rock Star, Dies," *Laconia Daily Sun*, March 27, 2020.
27. The Chaos and Kindness store relocated to the CAKE Theatre in downtown Laconia in May 2024. CAKE (the Chaos and Kindness Experience) is located at 12 Veterans Square.

Chapter 5

28. www.thefells.org.
29. Saint-Gaudens National Historical Park, www.nps.gov/saga.

Chapter 6

30. Historic Harrisville, www.historicharrisville.org.
31. *Red Brick Village*, a film by Ned Porter, Historic Harrisville, www.historicharrisville.org.

32. *American Ruins*, YouTube, 2018.
33. Lynne Borofsky, *Madame Sherri Revisited*, film, Chesterfield Historical Society, 2019.

Chapter 7

34. National Park Service, www.nps.gov.
35. Pierce Manse, www.piercemanse.org
36. See Laconia chapter, Belknap Mill.
37. Kathleen D. Bailey and Sheila R. Bailey, *Growing Up in Concord, New Hampshire: Boomer Memories from White's Park to the Capitol Theater* (Charleston, SC: The History Press, 2023), 136–37, "Old Railroad Station."
38. The first Brigade members were Polly B. Johnson, Carl Irving Bell, Anna and Bill Avery, George Keyes, Harold and Betty Yeaton and Ernest Freeman.
39. Polly B. Johnson, *The Pierce Brigade and the Crusade to Save the Home of Franklin Pierce, 14th President of the United States*, pamphlet.
40. Kathleen D. Bailey and Sheila R. Bailey, *New Hampshire War Monuments: The Stories Behind the Stones* (Charleston, SC: The History Press, 2022), 114–16.

Chapter 8

41. Warner House, www.warnerhouse.org.
42. Moffatt-Ladd House and Garden, www.moffattladd.org.
43. Wentworth-Gardner Historic House Association, www.wentworth-gardner.org.

Chapter 9

44. Manchester Historic Association, manchesterhistoric.org.
45. See *Norma Rae*, Twentieth-Century Fox, 1979.
46. Russell Dickerman died on August 7, 2024, at the age of ninety-four.
47. Steve Daly, *Dem Little Bums* (Plaidswede Publishing, 1993).
48. Barbara Ward, conversations, 2024.
49. See appendix I.

50. Bailey and Bailey, *New Hampshire War Monuments*, 21–22.

Chapter 10

51. Darryl Thompson, conversations, 2024.

Appendix I

52. These are the days, times and prices available at press time and may be subject to change.

ABOUT THE AUTHORS

KATHLEEN D. BAILEY is a journalist and novelist with forty years' experience in the nonfiction, newspaper and inspirational fields. Born in 1951, she was a child in the '50s, a teen in the '60s, a young adult in the '70s and a young mom in the '80s. While she's always dreamed of publishing fiction and has six novels in print, her three previous Arcadia projects—*Exeter: Past and Present*, *New Hampshire War Monuments* and *Growing Up in Concord, New Hampshire: Boomer Memories from White's Park to the Capitol Theater*—made her fall in love with nonfiction and telling real people's stories.

SHEILA R. BAILEY was a freelance photographer living in Concord, New Hampshire. She coauthored *Exeter: Past and Present*, 2021; *New Hampshire War Monuments: The Stories Behind the Stones*, 2022; *Growing Up in Concord, New Hampshire: Boomer Memories from White's Park to the Capitol Theater*, 2023; and *A History Lover's Guide to New Hampshire*, 2025. She provided the contemporary photos for the local history books written by Kathleen D. Bailey. She enjoyed traveling around New Hampshire and New England, searching for the perfect shot.